Relief

Meters	Feet
3050	10 000
1525	5000
610	2000
305	1000
152.5	500
Sea Level	0
	Below
	Sea Level
500	
5000	
10 000	

Goode's World Atlas, © Copyright 1987 by Rand McNally & Company,
R.L. 87-S-155

Arctic Circle

ARCTIC

Hammerfest

ICELAND

Reykjavik
Reykjanes
Hella

FÖNTUR

Tórshavn
FAEROE IS.
(Den.)

SHETLAND IS.
(Br.)
Lerwick

ORKNEY IS.
(Br.)

HEBRIDES

SCOTLAND
Moray Firth
GRAMPIAN MTS.
Aberdeen
Dundee

GLASGOW
BRITISH
Edinburgh
CHEVIOT HILLS

NORTHERN IRELAND
Belfast

IRELAND

Galway
Dublin
(Baile Átha Cliath)

Cork
Cobh

CAPE CLEAR

ISLES OF SCILLY

LANDS END

Carlisle

UNITED
ISLES
NEWCASTLE
KINGDOM

LIVERPOOL
LEEDS
MANCHESTER
Kingston upon Hull

BIRMINGHAM
Leicester
Southampton
Portsmouth
LONDON
Dover
Str. of Dover
Calais

English Channel
CHANNEL IS.
(Br.)
Cherbourg
Le Havre
Rouen

Brest
Rennes
PARIS

St. Nazaire
Orléans

Nantes
Tours

La Rochelle

FRANCE

Dijon

Bay of Biscay
Gironde

Bordeaux
Clermont-
Ferrand
MASSIF
CENTRAL
LYON

C. DE FINISTERRE
El Ferrol
La Coruña
Vigo
Porto
(Oporto)
Coimbra

Santander
Gijón
Oviedo
CORD. CANTABRICA
S. Sebastián
Bayonne
PYRENEES
Pico de Aneto
3404
ANDORRA

Bilbao

Salamanca
Valladolid
Douro
SIERRA DE
GUADARRAMA
MADRID
SPAIN

Zaragoza

Toulouse
Nîmes
MARSEILLE
Toulon

Golfe du Lion

BARCELONA
Tarragona
Tortosa

Valencia

LISBON
Lisboa
PORTUGAL

C. DE
SÃO
VICENTE

Cádiz
Sevilla
SIERRA MORENA
Guadalquivir
SIERRA NEVADA
Murcia
Cartagena

Gibraltar (Br.)
Almería
DEL ALBORÁN
(Sp.)

Málaga
Tanger
Ceuta (Sp.)
Tétouan
Oran

Rabat

Algiers
(Alger)

ISLAS BALEARES
MALLORCA
MENORCA
Palma
IBIZA
(Sp.)
C. DE LA
NAO

Bizerte

ATLANTIC OCEAN

NORTH
SEA

Bergen
Stavanger
Kristiansand
LINDESNES

Trondheim
(Nidaros)
DOVRE FJELL
Galdhøpiggen
2469

Oslo

Skagerrak
Ålborg

DENMARK
COPENHAGEN
(København)
Malmö

Kiel
HAMBURG
Bremen
Lübeck

NETHERLANDS
AMSTERDAM
The Hague
('s Gravenhage)
ROTTERDAM
ANTWERP
BELGIUM
BRUSSELS
LILLE
Lux.
LUXEMBOURG

Reims
Mainz a. M.
FRANKFURT a. M.
Nürnberg
STUTTGART

Strasbourg

Lausanne
Geneva
Bern
SWITZERLAND
Zürich

Mont Blanc
4807

MILAN
TURIN
Genoa
Nice
MONACO
La Spezia
Livorno
(Leghorn)

CORSICA
(Fr.)
Ajaccio

SARDINIA
(It.)

Cagliari

C. SPARTIVENTO

ROME
(Roma)

NAPLES
(Napoli)
Vesuvio
190

Palermo
Messina

TYRRHENIAN
SEA

IONIAN SEA

Norvik
Kebnekaise
2072

Luleå
Tornio
Oulu

Vaasa

Sundsvall

Gävle

STOCKHOLM
Uppsala
Karlstad
Norrköping
Göteborg
GOTLAND
Visby
ÖLAND

Turku
Helsinki

Hangö
Gulf of Finland
Tallinn
ESTONIAN S.S.R.
Tartu

Liepāja
LATVIAN S.S.R.
Jelgava
Riga
Daugavpils

Klaipeda
LITHUANIAN S.S.R.
Kaunas

Kaliningrad
R.S.F.S.R.
Vilnius

Gdańsk
Szczecin

GERMAN
DEM. REP.
BERLIN
Magdeburg
Poznań
Hannover
Leipzig
Dresden
FED.
REP.
OF GER.
COLOGNE
ESSEN
Bonn
Plzeň
PRAGUE
CZECHOSLOVAKIA
Brno
Ostrava

POLAND
WARSAW
Łódź
Lublin
Brest

Grodno
Białystok
Toruń
Baranovichi
Pinsk

KATOWICE
Kraków
Przemyśl
L'vov
Drogobych

VIENNA
(Wien)
AUSTRIA
Graz
Bratislava
BUDAPEST
HUNGARY
Szeged

Miskolc
Debrecen
Oradea
Cluj
ROMAN

Maribor
Ljubljana
Zagreb
Trieste
Venice
Bologna
Florence
Ancona
Zadar

Split
Sarajevo
YUGOSLAVIA
Novi Sad
Subotica

Belgrade

Dubrovnik
Cetinje
Shkodër
Durrës
Tirane
Bari
Brindisi

Zadar

BUCHAR

Danube
Sofia
(Sofiya)
BULG

Niš

Skopje
Bitola

GREECE
ATHENS
(Athínai)

MEDITERRANEAN

Enchantment of the World

BELGIUM

By Jim Hargrove

Consultant for Belgium: Aristide R. Zolberg, Ph.D., University-in-Exile Professor, New School for Social Research, New York, New York

Consultant for Reading: Robert L. Hillerich, Ph.D., Bowling Green State University, Bowling Green, Ohio

CHILDRENS PRESS ®

CHICAGO

A boat trip along the Meuse River passes old castles and fortresses.

Library of Congress Cataloging-in-Publication Data

Hargrove, Jim.
  Belgium.

  (Enchantment of the world)
  Includes index.
  Summary: An introduction to the geography, history, government, economy, culture, and people of this small country that is often called the ''crossroads of Europe.''
  1. Belgium—Juvenile literature. [1. Belgium]
I. Title. II. Series.
DH418.H37 1988   949.3   87-36753
ISBN 0-516-02701-8

Childrens Press, Chicago
Copyright ©1988 by Regensteiner Publishing Enterprises,
All rights reserved. Published simultaneously in Canada.
Printed in the United States of America.

  3 4 5 6 7 8 9 10 R 97 96 95 94 93 92 91 90

Photo Acknowledgments
Root Resources: ©Russel A. Kriete, Page 4; ©Grete Schiodt, Pages 27, 38; ©Jane H. Kriete, Page 36 (left)
©**Shostal:** Cover, Pages 5, 8, 33 (right), 89 (left), 91, 92 (right), 107, 110, 112, 115
©**Cameramann International, Ltd.:** Pages 6 (2 photos), 9, 11 (left top & bottom), 13, 22, 23 (right), 33 (left), 39 (2 photos), 60 (2 photos), 62 (left), 63, 65 (bottom left), 70 (2 photos), 86 (2 photos), 103 (left), 105 (right bottom), 106 (left), 114 (top left & bottom left)
©**Kirkendall/Spring:** Pages 10 (left), 25 (2 photos)

©**Mary Ann Brockman:** Pages 10 (right), 11 (right), 14 (left), 16 (2 photos), 20 (left), 23 (left), 26, 29, 30, 35 (2 photos), 36 (right), 40, 41 (2 photos), 65 (top), 66 (2 photos), 71, 75 (2 photos), 105 (left & top right), 106 (right)
©**Bob Skelly/Image Finders:** Pages 14 (right), 19 (2 photos), 24 (left), 44, 65 (bottom right), 72 (3 photos), 79 (right), 82, 89, (right), 103 (right), 114 (top right)
AP/Wide World Photos: Pages 15, 58, 59, 79 (left), 99 (right)
Journalism Services: ©John M. Nallon: Pages 20 (right), 108 (right)
©**Chip & Rosa Maria Peterson:** Pages 24 (right), 76
©**H. Armstrong Roberts:** Pages 47, 48 (right)
Historical Pictures Service, Chicago: Pages 48 (left), 50 (2 photos), 52 (2 photos), 54, 56, 92 (left), 94 (4 photos), 96, 99 (middle)
Valan Photos: ©Val & Alan Wilkinson: Pages 62 (right), 73 (right)
The Photo Source: ©Nick Meers: Page 67
Tom Stack & Associates: ©Hugh K. Koester: Page 73 (left), ©C. Benjamin: Page 111 (2 photos)
The Bettmann Archive: Page 99 (left)
The Third Coast Stock Source: ©Ted H. Funk: Pages 108 (left), 114 (bottom middle)
Chandler Forman: Page 114 (right)
Len W. Meents: Maps on pages 21, 40, 84
Courtesy Flag Research Center, Winchester, Massachusetts 01890: Flag on back cover
Cover: Typical Belgian village near Ypres

The Damme Canal connects Bruges with the sea at Zeebrugge.

TABLE OF CONTENTS

Above: A village in the Ardennes in the southeast
Below: A section of downtown Brussels

Chapter 1

BELGIUM: THE CROSSROADS OF EUROPE

Much of the excitement and glamor of western Europe seems to be packed into tiny Belgium. Not much larger than the state of Maryland, or Haiti in the West Indies, Belgium looks as if it were squeezed between its larger neighbors: France to the west, The Netherlands to the north, and Germany to the east. Only the tiny nation of Luxembourg on the southern border makes Belgium look large.

Belgium's size belies its importance to the culture and economy of western Europe. People traveling across the English Channel often arrive at or leave from Belgium. Overland travelers visiting Germany and The Netherlands almost certainly will pass through Belgium. Brussels, Belgium's capital city, is only a three-hour automobile drive from at least three other important European capitals: Paris, capital of France; Bonn, capital of West Germany; and The Hague, capital of The Netherlands.

Not surprisingly, Belgium is sometimes called the crossroads of Europe. The little nation has some of the finest highways, railroads, and ship waterways in the world. The first passenger train in Continental Europe began operating in Belgium in 1835.

The medieval, fortresslike Steen, now the Maritime Museum, which stands on the Schelde River in Antwerp, dates back to the tenth century.

Today, the Belgium national railroad crisscrosses the little country like a grid. Belgium has more railroad tracks per square mile than any other country in Europe.

The Belgian city of Antwerp, located on an inland finger of the North Sea, has one of the busiest seaports on the continent. Rivers and canals allow oceangoing ships to visit some of the cities in Belgium's interior. Even Brussels, nearly 100 miles (161 kilometers) away from the North Sea, has a canal that allows huge barges to dock at its port.

Partly because of its central location in western Europe, Belgium has become a center for industry and government offices. Brussels, especially, is host to some of the most important political organizations in the world. One of the largest and most interesting modern buildings in Brussels is the star-shaped *Berlaymont*. The Berlaymont building is the headquarters of the

Headquarters of the European Economic Community

European Economic Community (EEC), sometimes called the Common Market. In this huge office building, economic leaders from twelve different European nations, including Belgium, meet to improve industry and trade in their respective countries.

Brussels is also the home of the headquarters of NATO, the North Atlantic Treaty Organization. Nations that are members of NATO, including the United States, Canada, and many European countries, have agreed to work together to defend western Europe from attack by foreign powers.

People from many different nations work in the offices of NATO and the EEC. Therefore, it is not surprising to hear many different languages spoken on the streets of Brussels. But even outside of Brussels, few Belgians are surprised by the sound of foreign speech.

Windmills, many of which are standing today, were used to pump water out of the lowlands and into the canals that drained into the North Sea.

A NATION OF MANY LANGUAGES

Belgium has three official languages: Dutch (also called Flemish), French, and German. Most of the permanent residents of Belgium speak either Dutch or French.

Dutch-speaking Belgians are called Flemings. For the most part, Flemings live in the northern half of the country, the area of Belgium nearest The Netherlands. Flemings share many customs and beliefs with the Dutch-speaking citizens of The Netherlands. Even much of the land of northern Belgium is similar to The Netherlands. Along the coast of the North Sea, many dikes, or seawalls, have been built to hold back the water of the ocean, just as has been done for centuries in Holland. In Flemish Belgium, it is not surprising to see windmills and colorful flower farms, familiar sights in Holland as well.

Passing from east to west roughly through the center of Belgium is an invisible line that forms a legal boundary called the "Language Frontier." Almost all of the Flemish people live north of this invisible border. The portion of Belgium inhabited by the

The bilingualism of Belgium can be seen in menus, information signs, and even on television.

Flemish people is called Flanders. To the south live the Walloons, Belgian citizens who speak French. Southern Belgium is called Wallonia.

In many ways, the French-speaking Walloons resemble the people of France. Although the Flemish outnumber the Walloons by a ratio of five to three, a visitor to southern Belgium would never know that the Walloons were a minority. Here, the forested highlands abound with French road signs, newspapers, even French-speaking radio and television stations. In both Flanders and Wallonia, most radio and television stations are run by the Belgian government, but a few are independent.

A few German-speaking Belgians live in the eastern part of the country, near the border of West Germany. Although Belgium has a population of about 10 million, only about 1 percent, roughly 100,000 people, use German as their native tongue.

Of all the areas of Belgium, none has a greater diversity of languages than the capital city of Brussels. On the city's cable television network are four Belgian stations, three French, three German, two Dutch, two British, and even one from tiny Luxembourg.

From Flanders in the north to Wallonia in the south, Belgian citizens seem to take on many of the characteristics of their neighboring countries. One reason for this may be that Belgium has few natural borders. Rivers, oceans, and mountains often help mark national boundaries. Belgium's only natural border is a thirty-nine-mile (sixty-three-kilometer) stretch of land along the coast of the North Sea. No other bodies of water or high mountains separate Belgium from its European neighbors.

This lack of physical boundaries may help explain why so many Belgians seem to have been absorbed into the culture of their neighboring countries. It also may explain Belgium's significant— and often tragic—role in world history.

THE CROSSROADS OF HISTORY

Belgium did not become a nation until 1831, but was recognized much earlier as a distinct area of Europe. Many of the greatest battles in European and world history have been fought on Belgian soil. Near the city of Tongeren in the eastern part of the country, the Roman army of Julius Caesar fought thousands of Belgian soldiers during the Roman conquest of the huge area of Europe once called Gaul.

During the Middle Ages, the lands now within the borders of Belgium were invaded countless times. The people of Belgium often found themselves pawns in struggles between larger nations

Monument to the Battle of Waterloo

such as France, England, Spain, Austria, The Netherlands, and Germany.

In 1815, the French armies of the Emperor Napoleon were defeated at Waterloo, a small village just a few miles south of Brussels. The Battle of Waterloo was one of the most important events in European history because it ended the efforts of the French to build an empire in Europe.

Even in the twentieth century, huge battles have been fought in little Belgium. Many of the battles of World War I were fought in trenches dug into Belgian soil. One of the most famous engagements of World War II, the Battle of the Bulge, was fought in southeastern Belgium around Christmas in 1944. It signaled the beginning of the end of World War II in Europe.

Some of the largest military cemeteries in the world are in Belgium. With such a tragic history, it seems appropriate that the headquarters of NATO—the symbol of political security in western Europe—is located in Belgium.

Traffic on the main highway between Antwerp and Ghent, and bicycles parked in Bruges

THE OLD AND THE NEW, SIDE BY SIDE

There are less than twelve thousand square miles (a little more than thirty thousand square kilometers) of land in all of Belgium. Belgium is one of the most densely populated areas of Europe. Traveling by car on the excellent highways, even in the countryside, it is rare to be out of sight of a village or town.

The compact size of this diverse country adds much to its charm. In a matter of minutes, it is possible to drive from archaeological excavations, where important prehistoric finds have been made, to ancient Roman ruins, to magnificent cathedrals built in the Middle Ages, to some of the most modern buildings and factories in the world.

Riding in cars or in well maintained trams and buses on busy city streets, visitors can see bicyclists by the hundreds riding along specially marked bike lanes, often on both sides of the street. The city of Brussels has the most modern subway system in the world.

A painting of the 1973 coup in Chili, by artist
Roger Somville, is in a subway station in Brussels.

The subway trains (many passengers claim the cars have the most comfortable seats of any trains anywhere) pass beneath gorgeous buildings that are many centuries old.

But the spirit of old and new is preserved best, perhaps, by Belgium's many festivals. Few countries have as many celebrations as Belgium. And many of the festivals are much older than the nation itself.

The Belgians' enthusiasm for carnivals, parades, and processions seems to know no bounds. Most Belgians are Catholic, and many of the country's most important festivals are religious in origin. But almost any bit of history seems significant enough to begin decorating floats with flowers and putting on colorful costumes. There are festivals for historic battles, for trade guilds, for important religious events, even for cats!

Some festivals are so old that people can't seem to remember why they were started. It hardly matters. The rule of thumb seems to be: If in doubt, have a festival.

The Dutch-speaking Belgians, or Flemings, live in the
northern part of the country close to the North Sea.

Chapter 2

FLANDERS: THE NORTH COUNTRY AND THE FLEMINGS

Many visitors to Belgium learn to discuss the country's official languages carefully. All too soon, they find out that discussions about the differences between the Dutch-speaking northerners and the French-speaking southerners can lead to arguments. Flemings, the Belgian people who live in the northern part of the country and who speak Dutch, are in the majority in Belgium.

In the past, towns along the language frontier in central Belgium had great debates whether to adopt Flemish or French as the official language. Surveys were taken to determine how many people in a village spoke each of the two languages. The majority would determine the official language of the town. It was not unusual for a town to change its official language several times.

In 1962 and 1963, laws were passed making the language frontier permanent. Although villages in central Belgium no longer change their official languages, problems remain because people change the language they speak.

There is a great rivalry between the Flemings and the Walloons. Dutch and French are official languages of Belgium, but many residents of Flanders prefer to speak English rather than French to a visitor unable to understand the Dutch language. And few French-speaking Walloons enjoy learning the Dutch language of their cousins in the north.

It is not surprising that two large and very distinct cultures flourish in Belgium. There are, however, three areas in the nation where the cultures meet and mingle. One place is Brussels, the capital city; the second is along the language frontier; the last is the short strip of sandy beaches along the coast of the North Sea in Flanders.

BELGIUM'S COASTAL PLAYGROUND

In July and August, resort hotels along the seacoast of Belgium are crowded with vacationers from all parts of the little country, and from many other nations as well. The Belgian coast, from the border of France on the south to The Netherlands on the north, is virtually lined by an unbroken string of resort hotels and gambling casinos. During the peak of summer, the streetcars that run along the coast are crowded with vacationers visiting the beaches and resorts.

Although the tramway is close to the sea, riders traveling along its busy tracks see little of the water. High buildings and roads built over sand dunes block most of the view. On the inland side of the tramway are the *polders*, low-lying lands that have been reclaimed from the sea.

In the thirteenth, fourteenth, and fifteenth centuries, an extensive series of canals was built to drain the low-lying polders.

De Haan (left), a popular seacoast resort, and a canal built through the polders (right) near the North Sea

Windmills were used to pump water out of the lowlands and into the canals that drained into the North Sea. Many of these windmills and canals still exist.

In some areas along the Belgian coast, high sand dunes, some rising as much as sixty-five feet (twenty meters) above sea level, keep water from the North Sea out of the interior lowlands. Although the dunes play an important role in protecting the lowlands from the sea, many of them are now hard to recognize because they are covered by asphalt and cement. Where the sand dunes are not high enough, dikes and seawalls were built to keep the water from returning. Extending from ten to thirty miles (sixteen to forty-eight kilometers) inland, polders now account for about 10 percent of Belgium's total area.

The largest of the resort towns along the coast is Ostend, Belgium's oldest coastal community. Ostend's history dates back to the tenth century. From its port, the Crusaders set sail for the

Hotels and a fishing port in Ostend, the oldest settlement on the Belgian coast

Holy Land. In later centuries, the town became known as the queen of seaside resorts, because a number of European kings and queens vacationed there. Today, Ostend is famous for its wide beach, which runs the complete length of the town, a horse racing track, and a large casino. Just a few miles north of Ostend is the coastal resort of Knokke, which many Belgians regard as the most stylish of all the resorts on the North Sea Coast.

Ostend is also an important transportation center. Many people from England who intend to travel overland on the European continent first cross the English Channel and land at Ostend to begin their journey. A major European highway begins at Ostend and goes all the way to Istanbul, Turkey. A number of international trains traveling to many parts of Europe also start their journeys at Ostend. Belgium's short seacoast is well known to many European vacationers. The beach is covered with clean white sand almost entirely free of stones and, at low tide, nearly a half mile wide in some places. The seacoast of Flanders is a summer playground for Belgians as well, both Flemings and Walloons.

The climate throughout Belgium is cool and often rainy. In some parts of the nation, it rains as many as two hundred days

out of the year. The relatively short summers bring throngs of vacationers to the beaches of the North Sea. During winter, many of the shops, hotels, and casinos along the Belgian coast are closed, awaiting the return of the summer crowds.

THE PORT CITY OF ANTWERP

Although it is more than fifty miles (eighty kilometers) from the North Sea, the Schelde River and its estuaries have made Antwerp one of the most important ocean ports in the world. Belgians are extremely proud of the modern port at Antwerp. They sometimes boast that huge cargo ships can dock at Antwerp, load and unload their freight, and set sail again faster than at any other port. Covering an area of some 40 square miles (103 square kilometers), Antwerp's port is the fifth largest in the world.

Belgian workers improved the port at Antwerp by building the enormous Zandvleit lock, which was completed in 1967. The Zandvleit lock, the largest lock in the world, allows all oceangoing ships except for oil supertankers to dock at Antwerp.

The great docks along the Schelde River are relatively modern, but Antwerp is an ancient city. A portion of the old docks along the Schelde, called the *Quays*, was built in the nineteenth century by Napoleon. Firm knowledge about the city's history dates back to at least the seventh century. One of the oldest buildings still standing in Antwerp, Steen Castle, was built in the tenth century,

The Cathedral of Notre Dame contains three paintings by Peter Paul Rubens, who had his studio in Antwerp.

although many parts of it have since been rebuilt. It is now a museum.

Residents of Antwerp often call their city *La Métropole*, French for "the chief city." The inner part of the city, called by the Dutch name *Groote Markt*, or marketplace, contains many very old buildings. Most have been extremely well maintained.

The Cathedral of Notre Dame stands on the southeast side of Groote Markt. The great church was begun in 1352 and not completed until nearly two hundred years later. The restored cathedral is home for three masterpieces by the famous Belgian artist Peter Paul Rubens. Several other large churches were built in the city during the fifteenth and sixteenth centuries.

Although many historic buildings remain standing in Antwerp, much of the city was destroyed during World War II. In the final years of the war, Antwerp was a target of German V1 and V2 rockets. During the bombardments, many historic buildings were

The Groote Markt (left) and the Zandvleit lock, largest in the world (right)

damaged or destroyed, and about three thousand civilians were killed.

Despite the ravages of war, modern Antwerp is a commercial center of great importance. It has been the diamond-cutting capital of the world for nearly five hundred years. Today, about half the world's diamonds are cut, polished, and sold in Antwerp. A number of large factories employ thousands of people.

The rapid growth of Antwerp has caused the city to expand from its old site on the east banks of the Schelde to the west. Since 1969, automobile and railroad traffic has been able to cross under the wide river through the modern Kennedy Tunnel, opened that year. The Kennedy Tunnel helped the development of west Antwerp.

The grand mix of carefully preserved buildings and bustling commerce makes Antwerp one of the most important cities on the European continent.

Bruges is a medieval city with gabled buildings clustered around small squares or set in narrow streets.

OTHER HISTORIC FLEMISH CITIES

Traveling to the ancient city of Bruges is like taking a trip back in time. Located just a few miles southeast of Ostend, Bruges appears much as it did centuries ago. In the Middle Ages, Bruges was one of the largest and most important of all European cities. Its population then, about forty thousand, was as large as London's. It was famed as a port and a center where artisans made cloth.

During the fifteenth and sixteenth centuries, Bruges' Zwin River began to fill up with silt, and the city's great port eventually had to close. Oceangoing ships began using the port at Antwerp.

In modern times, the cobblestone streets and old buildings of Bruges have been carefully repaired and cleaned. People from all over the world now travel to Bruges to see how a great European city appeared during the Middle Ages. Sometimes called the Venice of the North, Bruges has an extensive network of

Because of its many canals, Bruges is called the Venice of the North.

*Ghent is built on a hundred islands formed
from branches of the Schelde and the Leie rivers.*

canals that runs through the city. Fifty bridges allow passage
across the water. Bruges, like a number of other old towns in
Flanders, is also famous for its art museums. It is hardly
surprising that tourism is the number-one industry in Bruges;
only Brussels attracts more tourists.

Another Flemish city noted for its historic buildings and art
museums is Ghent but, unlike Bruges, it is also a thriving
commercial center. Located where the Schelde and Leie rivers
meet, Ghent has the second largest port in Belgium. It is also a
mercantile center, where cloth, especially famous Belgian linen, is
manufactured. In Ghent, more than ten thousand people are
employed in weaving mills making the prized linen.

Many of Ghent's buildings are old and gray, but during much
of the year its streets are ablaze in color. As in Holland, there are

The Flower Market in Ghent

many flower gardens in Flanders, and Ghent is the capital of Belgium's flower industry. Many commercial flowers are grown in hothouses just outside the city. Throughout the year, brightly colored flowers also can be seen blooming along the ancient streets of the city.

THE FLEMISH COUNTRY

Belgium is the second most densely populated nation in Europe, and parts of Flanders are the most densely populated areas of Belgium. Traveling on the fine roads through Belgian pastures, farmlands, and flower fields, the sight of church steeples and castle turrets can be seen rising above the countryside.

The part of Flanders east of the Schelde River is often called *Kempenland*. Throughout much of this area the soil is poor and farms and villages are scarce. Although the soil makes farming difficult, Kempenland has huge deposits of coal and other minerals. Mining is an important industry in this area.

In all parts of Flanders, farms tend to be small. Under Belgian law, land is divided among the children of a family, making farms smaller and smaller as generations of farmers live on the same land. Many Flemish farms are no larger than three acres. Although less than 5 percent of Belgium's total population lives on farms, those who do are hardworking and efficient farmers. Flemish farmers carrying flashlights and lanterns can be seen scurrying across dark fields before the sun rises, ready to begin work. Because of the hard work of Belgian farmers, the country grows four-fifths of the food it consumes.

Belgium is a small country, and fertile farmland is valuable. Even land that is relatively poor is carefully fertilized and cared for by farmers who manage to grow crops where others would not even try. Much of the land in the Flemish countryside is used as grazing land for livestock, also.

Until the years immediately following World War II, most people in Flanders made their living working in the ports of the North Sea, on small farms, or by operating little shops, usually owned by a single family. In recent years, more and more Flemings have begun earning wages in factories, business offices, and large retail stores owned by corporations.

For more than a century, the Belgian government attempted to unify the Flemings and the Walloons, first by trying to persuade the entire country to speak French, and then by promoting bilingualism throughout the nation. But by the twentieth century, it was clear that separate Dutch- and French-speaking sections were a fact of life.

Livestock in the Flemish countryside

Flemish families, especially those living on farms or in small villages, tend to be larger than their counterparts in Wallonia. It is not unusual for a Flemish family to have four or more children. Many of these children are educated in Catholic schools supported by the government. Although most Belgians in both Flanders and Wallonia are nominally Catholic, the Flemish tend to go to church more regularly and to send their children to Catholic schools. Whether they go to Catholic or secular schools, Flemish children are instructed in the Dutch language, the official language of Flanders.

Flemings traditionally take both their work and recreational time very seriously. Small shops owned and operated by individual families are often open from very early in the morning to very late at night. Frequently, women and children work in the shops during the day while men work on their small farms. In the evening, the men will take turns working in the tiny stores.

By law, office and factory workers have forty-hour workweeks. Until recently, many workers were accustomed to taking long

Bicycling is enjoyed by everyone, including older people.

lunch breaks, often two hours or more. This custom is now in decline, but it indicates how seriously the Flemings regard eating.

Flemish meals, which emphasize meat and starchy vegetables such as potatoes, are served leisurely and in large quantities, as they are for Walloons. Many Flemish workers are prepared to spend a large percentage of their income on meat, which is quite expensive in Belgium.

Many Belgians, both Walloons and Flemings, are avid sports fans. Soccer is extremely popular throughout Belgium. In good weather, many Belgians enjoy making bicycle trips. Bicycle racing is a very popular sport, and takes place on outdoor tracks and roadways in the summer, and on indoor tracks in the winter. Racing champions are among the most important sports heroes in the country.

Chapter 3

WALLONIA: THE SOUTHERN HIGHLANDS AND THE WALLOONS

The French-speaking people who live in Wallonia, roughly the southern half of Belgium, look and act much like the people of France. Historically, the Walloons were often more strongly influenced by the people and culture of France than by the Flemish culture to the north. Many French kings were born and raised in the land that is now southern Belgium.

Some of the land in Wallonia is not suitable for farming, but there are rich deposits of coal and iron. For this reason, Belgium's first great factories were built not in Flanders but in Wallonia. During the eighteenth century, while Flemings were working on small farms and in little shops, many Walloons began working in huge factories where coal was burned to manufacture goods of iron and steel. Not until the 1950s did Flemish industry begin to catch up to the industries of Wallonia. Today, both northern and southern Belgium are highly industrialized.

Like The Netherlands, Belgium is often considered to be one of the Low Countries. Most of the land in Flanders is no more than a few hundred feet above the level of the North Sea, and some land is actually below sea level, protected by dikes. But the land of Wallonia is somewhat higher, some spots reaching well over 1,000 feet (305 meters) above sea level. Belgium's southern highlands are filled with forests, hills, and river valleys, and some of the loveliest land imaginable.

THE ARDENNES

One of the most beautiful areas of Belgium and of all Europe is located in the southern portion of Wallonia. The rolling hills and thick forests of southern Belgium are called the *Ardennes*. The forests of the Ardennes extend from France through southern Belgium and the little nation of Luxembourg and continue into West Germany.

Like the Belgian coast to the north, the Ardennes are a popular vacation spot for people from all over Europe. Although it is the least densely populated area of populous Belgium, the Ardennes are filled with resorts catering to vacationers. During the warm summer months, people travel to southern Belgium to enjoy hiking along carefully marked trails through the forested hills of the Ardennes, fishing and canoeing in fast streams that cut canyons through the lovely terrain.

The highest hill in the Belgian Ardennes, called Botrange, is just 2,275 feet (693 meters) above sea level. But many winter vacationers enjoy downhill skiing on the gentle slopes in southern Belgium. The area is also noted for cross-country skiing trails and hunting. Most hunters search for wild boar (a kind of pig locally called *sanglier*), deer, and rabbits. Extensive systems of caves are found under many of the hills of the Ardennes, and some people

Campers in a secluded valley of the Ardennes (left) and the city of Spa (right)

enjoy exploring them, even though it can be a dangerous sport!

Near the northeastern edge of the Belgian Ardennes is a little town called Spa. Nearly two thousand years ago, a Roman writer named Pliny the Elder noted that the natural springs around the area were often used to cure diseases. For centuries, people have traveled from all over Europe to drink and bathe in the mineral-rich water that bubbles out of the ground in many places around Spa. The name of the town gave rise to a new word in the English language, and in other languages as well. Today, the word "spa" describes resorts that have programs to improve health, often including mineral baths. There are thousands of spas in many nations of the world, and all were named after this little city at the edge of the Belgian Ardennes.

During the last three centuries, Spa has been visited by many of the kings and queens of Europe. In 1717, Czar Peter the Great made the long trip from Russia in the hope of curing attacks of indigestion. Today, visitors traveling south through Belgium often enter the Ardennes by way of Spa. There, they can walk along well trodden paths through the hills and forests of the northern Ardennes, stopping frequently to drink water from various springs. Many of the paths include what are called "PVs," an abbreviation that stands for the French words *points de vue,* or scenic lookouts. At PVs, tourists can enjoy spectacular views of the Ardennes countryside.

Some people claim that the water in Spa has nearly miraculous medicinal value, while most doctors throughout the world believe it is only of minimal value. But much of the scenery around Spa is so lovely that most visitors agree it can certainly cure low spirits.

The landscape of the Ardennes is extremely varied. Wide valleys, cut by rivers and streams, often snake through thick forests. In other spots, rocky ledges make plant growth almost impossible. Some other areas are swampy wastelands, seldom explored by people. Although the entire region is sparsely populated, little towns and ancient castles dot the landscape. Many visitors to the Ardennes avoid the expense of staying in hotels by camping out in the forests. It is not even necessary to own a car to explore the hilly countryside. As in every other area of Belgium, bus and train transportation is available for almost any imaginable destination. It is small wonder that the Belgian Ardennes have been a premier European vacationland for three centuries.

THE MEUSE VALLEY

The 560-mile- (901-kilometer) long Meuse River, one of the major waterways of Europe, begins in France, cuts through the southern half of Belgium, and continues northeastward into The

Cable cars carry visitors across the Meuse River to the Citadel (right).

Netherlands. The Meuse enters Belgium from France in the heart of the Ardennes, where it is a white-water stream tumbling down the hills through a narrow valley. As it leaves the Ardennes, the Meuse slows down and its banks widen. On either side, the estates of wealthy Walloons line the riverbanks, together with old castles, occasional churches, and an abundance of flowers. The Meuse continues to flow slowly northward through the lovely Wallonian countryside until it reaches the city of Namur, where it is joined by the Sambre River, which flows eastward from France.

The city of Namur is built on a hill overlooking the Sambre and Meuse rivers. At the very top of the hill is a huge mass of rock called the Citadel, where an old castle once inhabited by local nobility is located. Today, cable cars carry visitors to the top of the Citadel, where they can see a magnificent view of Namur, the Sambre and Meuse rivers, and the Wallonian countryside.

One of the most popular tourist attractions in Namur is the

A panorama of Namur (left) and the Sisters of Our Lady convent and church (right)

House of the Sisters of Our Lady, an old Catholic convent. The convent is filled with pictures and sculptures of religious themes, but one of the most peculiar scenes shows men jousting while standing on stilts. In the Middle Ages, jousting was a popular form of combat and sport. A jousting match involved two or more men standing or riding on horseback while carrying long lances, or spears. Men would run or ride toward each other and attempt to strike their opponent with the end of the lance. But in ancient Wallonia, people used to joust while standing on stilts!

One explanation for the strange practice is that the Meuse River frequently flooded, making walking for man or horse virtually impossible. But another story involves an ancient ruler named Jehan, duke of Namur. According to the legend, many years ago the people of Namur revolted against the rule of the duke. Angered by the revolt, Jehan surrounded the city with troops, keeping food away from the starving residents. When a group of people came to the duke seeking mercy, he angrily replied that he would see no one traveling "on foot, horse, cart, or boat."

According to the legend, some imaginative residents of the city then walked to the duke's castle on stilts. When he saw the tall group of people seeking food, the duke was reportedly amused enough to take mercy on the residents of the city. The tradition of walking and jousting on stilts was carried on for many years during festivals and sporting events in Namur.

At the city of Namur, often called the gateway of the Ardennes, the Meuse River turns eastward, and flows toward The Netherlands and Germany. This long stretch of the Meuse is highly industrialized. Barges carrying coal and steel goods sail up and down the wide river, made considerably larger after being joined by the water of the Sambre. Brick factories and industrial railroad tracks frequently can be seen along the banks. As the Meuse River approaches the large city of Liège, it flows through the heart of industrial Wallonia. Eventually, it again turns northward and, for a few miles, flows between Belgium and The Netherlands before continuing northward into The Netherlands, where its name becomes the Maas. Eventually, it empties into the North Sea.

LIÈGE, THE CAPITAL OF WALLONIA

Liège, the largest city in Wallonia and the third largest in Belgium, is built on the banks of the Meuse River. For many years, Liège was the industrial and coal mining center of the nation, but now its steel mills and factories must compete with newer ones in Brussels and Antwerp to the north. Nevertheless, much of Liège's character is industrial. Abandoned coal mine shafts are scattered throughout the area, and the flaming chimneys of steel mills have given Liège the nickname "the burning city."

A view of Liège

At Liège, the Meuse River becomes extremely wide and is filled with islands. Huge industrial barges float on the broad water alongside brightly colored sailboats and pleasure craft. Modern Liège is noted today as much for its tourist business and lively nightlife as it is for its industry. Liège is also the most controversial city in Belgium.

Many of the people who live in and around Liège hold strong political beliefs. There tend to be more political demonstrations and arguments in Liège than anywhere else in Belgium.

For centuries, Liège has been a capital for the firearms industry. The gunsmiths of Liège have been recognized as masters of the craft virtually since the birth of firearms. The Armorer's Museum exhibits guns made in Liège for six centuries, from ancient muskets to modern machine guns.

But Liège has more to offer the visitor than riotous, strong political beliefs and the armaments trade. Birthplace of the well-known classical music composer César Franck, Liège is the host of

Left: César Franck Street in the hilly section of Liège
Right: From Liège, the Albert Canal winds to the North Sea.

a number of great museums and other cultural institutions, most of which are located in the small Old City of Liège, with buildings dating back to the 1600s. Little exists in the city that is any older, because Liège was completely destroyed in 1468 by the troops of Charles the Bold, duke of Burgundy. The duke spared only a few churches, some of which still stand today.

Despite the disaster of centuries ago, as well as additional damage suffered during both World Wars in the twentieth century, Liège remains a fascinating place to visit. Many neighborhoods are covered with dingy soot from factories. The dark waters of the Meuse meander through much of the city, and spacious wooded parks are abundant. Many visitors remark that the residents are particularly friendly and that the culture, despite the closeness of the German border, is the most decidedly French of any area in Wallonia.

Much of Tournai was damaged by bombs during World War II, but the Cathedral of Notre Dame escaped damage.

WESTERN WALLONIA

In the open fields of western Wallonia, agriculture and industry exist side by side. Farming is often done on a large scale, much different from the small, family-run farms found in Flanders. Most of the wheat and other grains used in Belgium are grown on the big, efficient farms of western Wallonia. But this is also an area of coal mining and iron manufacturing. In some places, huge piles of slag, the glassy residue left over when iron is removed from its ore, can be seen between the wheat fields.

At the western edge of Wallonia, near the French border, is the ancient city of Tournai. Present-day Tournai was conquered by the Roman armies of Julius Caesar about two thousand years ago. Although few relics of the Roman occupation remain, some of the buildings in Tournai are remarkably old. The enormous and beautifully maintained Cathedral of Notre Dame, in the very center of the town, dates from 1030, although some parts were built as late as the thirteenth century.

Rue Barre Saint-Brice (left) in Tournai and a narrow, hilly street (right) in the old section of Mons

A number of buildings in central Tournai were built in the twelfth and thirteenth centuries. The oldest private houses still standing on the continent of Europe are located at 10 and 12 rue Barre Saint-Brice, in Tournai. Both structures were built in 1175.

The Schelde River passes through Tournai. From the many bridges spanning the river, pedestrians can watch big barges traveling from central France to Antwerp and The Netherlands.

Another important city in western Wallonia is Mons, located about thirty-five miles (fifty-six kilometers) southwest of the capital city of Brussels. Like Liège to the east, Mons is in the center of an old coal mining district, although all mining operations within the city ceased in 1976.

In Latin, Mons means "hill," and Mons is a very hilly city. Nearly two thousand years ago, Roman soldiers built a fortress at Mons so they could overlook the surrounding countryside. Even in the final decades of the twentieth century, Mons is an important city for soldiers from many countries of the world. About 15 percent of the population of the city is employed at SHAPE, which stands for Supreme Headquarters Allied Powers in

Europe. The huge SHAPE building, and an entire village built up around it, are located just five miles (eight kilometers) north of Mons on the road to Brussels. At SHAPE are military leaders, workers, and their families from all the nations belonging to NATO. About three-quarters of the people who work at SHAPE speak English. Because more than two thousand families of SHAPE personnel live in and around Mons, English is an important second language in this area of Wallonia.

THE WALLOONS

As in the northern districts of Flanders, some children in Wallonia go to schools run by the Catholic church. But far more Walloon children attend secular schools than do children in Flanders. Whether they are taught by nuns and monks in Catholic schools or by public schoolteachers, almost all students in Wallonia learn French as their primary language.

The overwhelming majority of Belgians are Catholic, in Wallonia as well as in Flanders, but the Walloons tend to take religion less seriously than the Flemings. Only about one-third of the Walloon population attends church every week. For reasons that are not entirely clear, the Walloon birthrate is among the lowest in the world. As opposed to the Flemings, whose families usually include two, three, and four children, the average Walloon family has but a single child.

Belgium is a relatively well-to-do nation, and most Belgian families have at least one car. But many Belgian cities, including those in Wallonia, are very old and have narrow streets that were originally built for pedestrians and horse-drawn carriages. Driving a car in the old sections is often very difficult.

Workers in Wallonia have faced a number of problems in the second half of the twentieth century. The rich coalfields around Liège and Mons began to be used up after years of intense mining. Coal became more difficult and expensive to mine. At the same time, industrial centers in Flanders, especially around Antwerp and Brussels, began to develop quickly. With more modern factories than those found in Wallonia, Flemish manufacturers were soon able to produce some goods more efficiently than the Walloons. Unemployment in Wallonia rose as the demand for labor increased in Flanders.

The future for Wallonia is not entirely bleak. Nuclear power plants have replaced many coal-burning furnaces to produce electricity. While it is difficult to manage the tiny farms in Flanders efficiently, many of the much larger farms in Wallonia are run according to the most modern principles of agriculture.

THE NATION OF BELGIUM

The land that is now Belgium has been the scene of countless battles for thousands of years. The independent nation of Belgium was not born easily, and there are few Belgians today who would not defend the integrity of their country against the influences of their larger neighbors.

At the same time, however, the pressures that exist between the Flemish and Walloons make national unity difficult to achieve. A number of historians have compared the Belgians to members of a family who frequently argue among themselves but forget their quarrels and show a unified front when they deal with the rest of the world. Belgium is a peculiar as well as a lovely and richly historical nation.

*The castle of the Counts of Flanders in Ghent was built in
the twelfth century, modeled after forts used by the Crusaders.*

Chapter 4

TWO THOUSAND YEARS OF STRUGGLE

Belgium is as rich in history and historical treasures as any country on earth, and yet it did not become an independent nation until 1831. Because of its strategic location at the center of western Europe, and a lack of natural boundaries such as mountains and rivers to protect it, the land that is now Belgium has suffered countless invasions from Biblical times right into the twentieth century.

Over a period of nearly two thousand years, Belgium has been ruled by Rome, Spain, Austria, France, The Netherlands, and Germany, among others. Even the name Belgium, once used by Julius Caesar around 50 B.C., was soon forgotten and not used again to describe the modern nation until the nineteenth century. The story of the rise of modern Belgium is long and often tragic.

ANCIENT GAUL

In the years before the birth of Christ, the Roman Empire conquered much of Europe. In 57 B.C., and again in 53 B.C., Roman soldiers under the command of Julius Caesar attacked the tribes of settlers who were living in the land now called Belgium.

This first of many great wars fought on Belgian soil must have been a savage one. The land that is now made up of France, Belgium, and some other regions was called *Gaul* by the early Romans. Caesar wrote that the people he called the *Belgae* were "the bravest of all the Gauls." After 53 B.C., the land that is now Belgium became part of the Roman Empire, which at its height around A.D. 117 completely surrounded the Mediterranean Sea.

THE FRANKS SETTLE IN FLANDERS

The people Julius Caesar called the Belgae were actually Celts, people who had lived in what is now Great Britain and France. But in the third century A.D. a new tribe of people, called Franks, moved from Germany and settled in the land that is now Flanders. At the time, Christianity was spreading throughout the Roman world, but the Franks neither became Christian nor learned the language and customs of the Romans.

By the third century A.D., the language divisions of modern Belgium were already becoming established. In the north, the Franks continued to use Germanic speech patterns that eventually evolved into Dutch. In the south, the Celts developed a language based on the patterns of Latin speech, the ancient language of the Romans, and eventually transformed it into French. The language frontier that was established in the third century has been altered only slightly up to the present day.

In the fifth century, the Roman Empire collapsed, and the era of Roman rule over Belgium came to an end. With the powerful armies of Rome rapidly disappearing, new waves of Franks entered northern Belgium. For a time, Frankish rulers were extremely powerful.

*An engraving
showing Clovis
punishing a rebel*

BELGIUM DURING THE MIDDLE AGES

In 465, a Frankish nobleman named Clovis was born in
Tournai, in present-day Wallonia. Clovis became a Christian
before his thirtieth birthday, but the change had little effect on his
desire to conquer land. Before the end of the century, Clovis left
Tournai for France, where he eventually conquered an empire that
stretched from Germany through Belgium and across northern
France.

The descendants of Clovis were not as strong as the original
conqueror, and for two centuries various groups of people fought
for control of central Europe. Gradually, local Frankish noblemen
began to assume greater amounts of power. One of them, Pepin
the Short, the son of the Frankish ruler Charles Martel, owned
vast amounts of land in the Meuse valley near Liège, which in the
eighth century was just a tiny village.

Pepin the Short (left) and Charlemagne (right)

In 741 or 742, Pepin the Short's son, soon to be known throughout most of Europe as Charlemagne, was born. Upon the death of Pepin the Short in 768, Charlemagne and his brother Carloman became rulers of the Frankish kingdom. Carloman died in 771, leaving Charlemagne as the sole ruler of an empire that included most of present-day France, West Germany, The Netherlands, Austria, and Belgium.

Under the rule of Charlemagne, people living within today's Belgian borders enjoyed decades of relative peace. Although gold was scarce and trade and commerce existed only locally, some of the ancient Belgian trades began to flourish again. In the north country, skilled workers began making and selling fine cloth, a trade still practiced in Flanders. In southern Belgium, skilled workers renewed their trade in metal goods. But this era of peace was relatively short-lived.

Charlemagne died in 814, and his empire was finally divided into three different parts in 843. Without a strong ruler to defend it, Belgium was attacked by invaders from the north. Sailing in fearsome warships from their homes in Scandinavia, Viking

Norsemen sailed down the Schelde and Meuse rivers in Belgium, and the Rhine River in Germany, attacking and looting anything they felt was of value. In France, Belgium, and Germany, people were terrorized by the Viking raids. Churches and towns were destroyed, their treasures looted. Many Celt and Frankish people were carried away to become Viking slaves.

French and German kings, the supposed protectors of the land, were unable to defend their subjects from the dreaded Norse invasions. Once again, local noblemen—dukes and counts—rose to defend the land that kings were unable to protect. In northwestern Belgium, the counts of Flanders built huge castles and organized armies to defend their land against Viking attacks. The dukes of Brabant, the counts of Hainaut, and the prince-bishop of Liège attained great power in other areas of Belgium, building great castles, erecting stone walls around cities, and rebuilding ravaged churches. Very gradually, the threats from Viking warriors decreased.

Although Belgium was a fragmented land during the Middle Ages, many of its oldest architectural treasures date from that era. A number of great cathedrals and castles that were built during this period still stand, even though many others were destroyed in the world wars of the twentieth century.

Near the end of the Middle Ages, around the thirteenth and fourteenth centuries, everyday life in Belgium, as in other parts of Europe, began to change. Medieval towns began to develop, often in areas that had served as headquarters for the rising merchant class. Some merchants and tradesmen obtained charters from local noblemen to give the new towns an official status. Large and powerful associations, often called "guilds," were developed by skilled craftsmen.

Stonemasons and spinners during the Middle Ages

The clothmakers of Flanders and the metalworkers of the southern areas became a strong and influential class of tradesmen, gradually rivaling the peasant farmers and serfs who had toiled on tiny farms in earlier centuries. By the end of the thirteenth century, nearly half the people in Flanders worked in industry, a surprising percentage in this era well before the start of the Industrial Revolution. During this same period, many of the Flemish lowlands were drained and dikes were built so that larger and more efficient farms could be established to feed the growing population. It was a relatively peaceful time, but it wouldn't last. In little more than a century, Belgium once again became a battleground, a situation that existed on and off for five hundred years.

THE BATTLEGROUND OF KINGS

In 1369, Philip the Bold, duke of French Burgundy, married Margaret of Male, the only child of the count of Flanders. When the count died fifteen years later, Burgundy (today a section of

France) and Flanders were united. Within a few more years, almost all of the land that is now Belgium, as well as The Netherlands, came under control of the duke of Burgundy and was called the "Burgundian Netherlands."

Throughout the first seventy-five years of the 1400s various dukes of Burgundy ruled the land. Called "The Great Dukes of the West" and regarded by many as kings, the Burgundian dukes ruled over a golden age in Belgian history. Many of the nation's greatest architectural and artistic masterpieces were created in the fifteenth century. But the grand age came to an end in 1477, when the last of the Burgundian dukes, Charles the Bold, was defeated and killed in battle by forces of the king of France.

The French king sent a message to Mary of Burgundy, the heir of Charles the Bold. She must, the king demanded, marry his oldest son, and in that way join the Burgundian Netherlands with France. Mary knew that her badly beaten armies had little chance to defend Flanders from attack by the powerful armies of France. A quick marriage seemed the only answer. But instead of agreeing to marry the heir to the French throne, Mary wrote to Maximilian of Austria, son of that nation's emperor, and proposed marriage. Maximilian of Austria and Mary of Burgundy were married in 1477, the same year Mary's father was killed.

Mary of Burgundy had married into the powerful Hapsburg dynasty of Austria, which, by 1515 under Charles V, ruled one of the largest empires the world has ever known. It included most of Europe from Spain to Hungary, with the exception of France, as well as the recent huge land claims of Spain in the New World. Belgian historians like to point out that Charles V was born in Ghent in Belgium and raised in another Belgian city, Mechelen.

Charles V spent much of his forty-year reign commanding

Charles V (left) and Maximilian and his bride, Mary of Burgundy (right)

armies to defend his colossal empire. But as the years went by, an even more serious threat to his power began to develop right in his own backyard. This was the age of Martin Luther, John Calvin, and the Protestant Reformation. Thousands of Belgians, as well as other Europeans, were leaving the sometimes corrupt Catholic church to join the new Protestant cause. Charles V, like the other Hapsburgs, considered himself a devout Catholic. When Protestants were found worshiping in hidden locations, especially in the forests around Belgian cities, he sent armies to arrest them.

During the final years of his reign, Charles V spent much of his time trying to put down the new Protestant movement. By 1555, he was so tired and saddened by the effort that he decided to give up his throne so that his son, Philip of Spain, could become the new emperor. But as soon as Philip took power, religious violence broke out on a large scale in the land now called the "Spanish Netherlands." Violent Protestants broke into Catholic churches all over Belgium, smashing and burning many of their contents.

After some years of scattered violence, Philip finally sent an army of ten thousand Spaniards to crush the religious revolt in the Lowlands. Philip's forces imprisoned thousands of people, and cut off the heads of hundreds of others, including a number of popular Flemish noblemen. Other members of the Flemish nobility, many of them recently turned Protestant, organized armies to fight Philip's Spanish troops and to seek independence for the Spanish Netherlands. The war that had started is known as the "Revolt of the Netherlands."

Between 1568 and 1648, a period of eighty years, there was nearly continuous warfare in the Spanish Netherlands. In 1576, an army of Spanish soldiers killed thousands of the residents of Antwerp, only a small fraction of them soldiers, in a bloodbath that became known as the "Spanish Fury." At various times, troops surrounded the Belgian cities of Ypres, Bruges, Ghent, Brussels, and Antwerp, keeping food and other necessities from reaching the residents. Many people starved. Smaller cities were burned and totally destroyed. Terrified civilians fled by the thousands to Germany, France, and Great Britain, and especially to the north to what is now The Netherlands, where the rebels were successful.

By 1648, much of Europe had been involved in three decades of fighting, the conflict that became known as the Thirty Years' War. But, for the land that is now called Belgium, war had been raging for a half century longer. By 1648, however, the entire continent was exhausted by the long, partially religious struggle. A treaty was made to solve the problems between Protestants and Catholics in the Spanish Netherlands. The territory was recognized as being independent, and the northern area became the nation of The Netherlands. The southern area—today's

The Battle of Waterloo

Belgium—remained under the control of Spain. This agreement, made more than three centuries ago, explains why Belgium is a strongly Catholic nation today.

For nearly the next two centuries, Belgium was invaded, and ruled, by one European power after another. Spanish, Austrian, French, and Dutch rulers came for a time, were usually driven out in fierce battles, and replaced by new rulers. In 1790, the Belgians rebelled against the Austrian government and proclaimed their country's independence; but this revolution was put down by force.

One of the fiercest battles of all was Waterloo. A field outside the little Belgian town just south of Brussels was the final battleground for France's emperor, Napoleon Bonaparte, whose armies were defeated there in 1815 by the English and Prussians. As was so often the case, wars fought in Belgium were sometimes between other nations merely using the land as a battlefield. When the empire built by Napoleon finally crumbled in Belgium, there was a chance for Belgian independence, but it still would not happen for fifteen years.

Following the defeat of Napoleon, Belgium and The Netherlands, by international agreement, were joined to become the kingdom of The Netherlands. The Belgians were not consulted on this. Prince William of Orange, a Dutchman and a Protestant, became William I, the first king of the new nation. Belgium was still controlled by a foreign power, but the long struggle for independence was at last coming to an end.

THE BIRTH OF BELGIUM

By 1828, thousands of Belgians were seeking, if not independence, at least more control of their own land, separate from The Netherlands. By the following year, a petition seeking more local rights had been signed by about 300,000 Belgians. Soon, performances of popular plays and operas in Brussels and elsewhere began to be spiced with emotional calls for liberty. By August of 1830, large-scale disturbances broke out. Outnumbered, troops of King William I fled, allowing a citizen's group to set up a temporary government in Belgium.

Failing to understand the size of the revolt, the king sent a small group of soldiers to Brussels to try to put down the resistance. But volunteer soldiers from throughout Flanders and Wallonia were already flocking to Brussels, many carrying the red, yellow, and black flag that symbolized revolution and freedom. By September 26, 1830, after three days of fighting in and around the streets of Brussels, the king's troops were driven out and pursued to Antwerp, which they occupied on October 2. In a matter of days, they were driven out of Antwerp, although Dutch soldiers kept

Leopold I,
the first king
of Belgium

control of a portion of high land, from which they bombarded the
city. On October 4, 1830, the revolutionary government declared
Belgium an independent nation, and called for a meeting to write
a constitution.

Fearing the outbreak of a wider war, representatives from a
number of powerful European nations met in Great Britain to
discuss the problems in Belgium. The representatives eventually
agreed to dissolve the kingdom of The Netherlands and establish
Belgium as an independent country. The most powerful nations of
Europe had approved the formation of the nation of Belgium. In
February 1831, the revolutionary government of Belgium chose
their first king, Leopold I, a German prince who was an uncle of
Britain's Queen Victoria. The Belgians who fought for
independence from The Netherlands were great admirers of the
United States and insisted on having a written constitution that
limited the powers of government. This was very unusual for
Europe at the time. According to the constitution, although he
was king, Leopold I had to govern in accordance with the wishes
of Parliament. Members of Parliament were elected, but only by

the richer section of the population. After at least two thousand years of struggle, Belgium was at last free and independent.

The remainder of the nineteenth century was relatively peaceful. In 1865, Leopold II, a shrewd businessman, became the new king of Belgium. Leopold II organized expeditions of Belgian explorers and settlers to the valley of the Congo River in Africa, where a Belgian colony was established. Until the area became independent in 1960, the natural resources of the Belgian Congo added immeasurably to the wealth of the little European nation.

BELGIUM IN THE TWENTIETH CENTURY

In its relatively short history, Belgium has had only five kings: Leopold I, Leopold II, Albert I, Leopold III, and Baudouin I, the current monarch. During the latter half of the nineteenth century and throughout most of the twentieth, Belgium has been a prosperous nation. But even in the twentieth century, tragedy has returned to the country.

In 1914, at the start of World War I, German troops swept through Belgium on their way to France. By the end of the year, only three Belgian towns were free of German rule. Under the personal command of Albert I, who was called the "soldier king," the Belgians managed to keep control of a tiny portion of their nation until the Allied forces advanced through Belgium near the end of the war in 1918. The little country suffered terribly throughout World War I. Aid to "starving Belgium" became a battle cry throughout the free world. More than eighty thousand Belgians were killed during the war.

On May 10, 1940, history was tragically repeated. With no warning whatsoever, the Nazi air force of Adolf Hitler bombed

During World War II, Allied soldiers used sleds to transport supplies in the Ardennes.

Belgian communication centers, railroad stations, and airports. At the same time, German soldiers parachuted onto Belgian soil in huge numbers. Eight days later, the Belgian king, Leopold III, surrendered to the overwhelming Nazi forces and was taken prisoner. Many Belgians were killed during the cruel German invasion. During the German occupation, about eighteen thousand Belgians were sent to concentration camps, where many died.

In 1944, the Allied forces under the command of United States General Dwight Eisenhower were advancing across Europe toward Germany. In a desperate attempt to stop the advance, the German army attacked the Allied line in the beautiful Ardennes forests of southern Wallonia in mid-December. Probably because it was so thickly forested, Allied forces in the Ardennes were thin. The Germans quickly broke through the Allied lines, forming a "bulge" of German control some fifty miles (eighty kilometers) into the Belgian forest, and began marching toward Namur and Liège.

One of the largest battles in world history followed, the famous Battle of the Bulge. Once again, the great powers of the world were in mortal combat on Belgian soil. By the end of January

Bastogne, in the Ardennes, after the Battle of the Bulge in 1945.

1945, the Allied forces had won, and 220,000 German soldiers were dead. It was the decisive European battle of World War II.

At the conclusion of the conflict, war-ravaged Belgium once again had to pull itself together. Many of the nation's historic buildings had been destroyed, and the economy was in a shambles. But prosperity eventually returned, and Belgium enjoyed a remarkable business boom during the 1960s. In the late 1970s and 1980s, like much of the rest of the world, the Belgian economy suffered a business crisis, with high unemployment and rising prices.

The history of Belgium is far grander than its size would indicate. In this tiny jewel of the European continent, it is still possible to see reminders of its tragic history. In many of its ancient churches, one can see empty spaces that once held religious statues that were smashed during the Reformation in the sixteenth century. Although massive rebuilding efforts have been made, evidence of the damage from two world wars can still be seen in some cities. But perhaps the most tragic sight of all is the countless cemeteries that dot the Belgian landscape, a sad reminder of generations of people—Belgians and foreigners alike—who gave their lives to centuries of warfare.

The Grand' Place,
or marketplace, (left)
and pedestrians at
a busy intersection
(above) in Brussels,
the capital of Belgium

Chapter 5

BRUSSELS: THE CAPITAL OF EUROPE

In Belgium, it seems as if almost all roads lead to Brussels, the capital city, and it is easy to understand why. Brussels is one of the most beautiful and important of all the cities of Europe. It is also a city of astonishing contrasts, where ancient buildings and narrow cobblestone streets can be found next to modern, gleaming skyscrapers.

Officially, Brussels is the capital of Belgium, but is has been called by many the capital of Europe. Actually, the municipality of Brussels is just one of the nineteen districts that make up the metropolitan area, but most people refer to the entire area as Brussels. Of the more than one million people who live in Greater Brussels, one-fourth are foreigners. Some of the foreigners work in the huge buildings that form the headquarters of NATO and the European Economic Community. Others work for large, multinational corporations with offices in the city. Still others are North African immigrants who came to the Brussels area to do jobs requiring tough, physical labor.

Although Brussels is located in southern Flanders, it is a bilingual city; its government recognizes two languages. Street

Bilingual street signs and a tram

signs, advertisements, and all sorts of written messages are printed both in Dutch and in French. And because so many foreigners live in Brussels, almost any language imaginable can be heard in public places. In many hotels, restaurants, and stores, English is spoken nearly as often as the native languages of Belgium. As much as any metropolis in the world, Brussels is an international city.

Brussels is filled with superb restaurants and charming outdoor cafes, where an elegant meal or a simple snack can be purchased. The city also is host to several of the finest art museums in the world, as well as magnificent buildings that are centuries old.

Completed in the early 1980s, Brussels' subway system is the most comfortable and modern in Europe. Most of its stations are decorated with enormous and often highly unusual and original artworks. Passengers traveling below the city streets sit in soft, plush seats and listen to recorded music. In contrast to the modern subway system are the old trams, or streetcars, that run up and down many streets in the city. Brussels is one of the few great cities in Europe that has preserved its system of trams.

One of the many outdoor cafes in Brussels

For this rich mixture of modern glamor and historical charm, the visitor to Brussels must pay a price. The better restaurants and hotels in the city usually cater to people working for business or government organizations. Their workers often pay their bills from expense accounts maintained by their offices. For private tourists on vacation in Brussels, the holiday can be very expensive!

THE GRAND' PLACE

Brussels is an ancient city. According to legend, Charlemagne greeted Pope Leo III in the year 804 in Brussels. By the tenth century, it had become an important trading center for merchants traveling between France and Germany. Like other cities that developed during the Middle Ages, it has a centrally located public square, or market. But Brussels' square, called the Grand' Place, has an unusual history.

63

In the fifteenth, sixteenth, and seventeenth centuries, glorious buildings were erected, many by wealthy trade guilds, around the public square. On some days, brightly colored banners were hung from the buildings and important city officials and tradesmen would parade around the square wearing their finest clothes. But near the end of the seventeenth century, disaster struck.

In 1695, armies of the French king Louis XIV were trying to conquer the land. The French were trying to capture the city of Namur, but the armies of other nations, including England, Sweden, Holland, Austria, and Germany were trying to stop the French. To take attention away from the battle at Namur, Louis XIV ordered his army to destroy Brussels. The French soldiers brought dozens of cannons and other huge guns to the outskirts of the city and bombarded it for forty-eight hours with cannonballs heated in a fire until they were red hot.

Throughout Brussels, more than two thousand houses and other buildings were destroyed. The entire Grand' Place, except for the Town Hall, was leveled. But the hearty residents of Brussels refused to allow the center of their city to be a shambles. In less than four years, they completely rebuilt the Grand' Place, making it even more elegant than before. By 1699 they had completed one of the most grand and beautiful sights in all Europe, the new Grand' Place of Brussels.

As opposed to the square that had been destroyed, the rebuilt Grand' Place was constructed according to a plan that makes the rows of fancy buildings even more impressive. The tops and fronts of the buildings have many ornate sculptures and fancy areas of scrollwork. Parts of many of the buildings are covered with gold leaf.

Town Hall, called the *Hôtel de Ville* in French, was built in the

Top: Ommegang is a festival celebrated in July in the Grand' Place. Above and left: The Hôtel de Ville, or Town Hall, built in the fifteenth century, is the highlight of the Grand' Place.

The buildings in the Grand' Place represent different trade guilds and are decorated with gold-scrolled facades.

early 1400s under the direction of the dukes of Burgundy. It is the only building in the Grand' Place not completely destroyed in 1695. The building is topped by a tall, thin tower that contains a statue of St. Michael, the patron saint of Brussels. Inside are large oil paintings of many Belgian rulers and officials of Brussels, and rich tapestries created during the reigns of the dukes of Burgundy.

Most, but not all, of the other buildings in the Grand' Place were built for the old trade guilds: butchers, masons, cabinetmakers, brewers, hatmakers, and so on. Some of Brussels' most elegant restaurants and picturesque cafes are located in these old buildings, and in other buildings near the Grand' Place. The importance of trade organizations and labor unions in Belgium continues to this day. Nearly all of today's Belgian workers belong to powerful labor unions. There are also associations for independent professionals and businesspeople.

The Grand' Place floodlit at night

One of the square's great buildings that was not built by an old trade guild is the *Maison du Roi* (House of the King), which was originally built in the sixteenth century by Charles V to house a number of government offices. The building holds a large city museum containing many fascinating exhibits, including paintings nearly five hundred years old.

Since 1972, cars and trucks have not been allowed to park along the Grand' Place, and at night the buildings are brightly lit with floodlights. At any time, but especially at night, the Grand' Place is a beautiful sight. Because historic buildings completely surround the center square, a visitor to the Grand' Place cannot see any modern buildings. It is almost like stepping into a time machine.

Just a few winding blocks away from the Grand' Place, directly behind the Town Hall, is the most famous statue in Brussels. Only about two feet (sixty-one centimeters) tall, the little bronze boy called the *Manneken Pis* stands above a fountain where, for centuries, he has followed nature's call. Created in 1619 by Jerome Duquesnoy, the nude statue of a little boy urinating is a long-time favorite among residents of Brussels and visitors as well. He has been stolen often as a prank, and even more often is clothed in a variety of costumes. More than four hundred outfits for the *Manneken Pis* are kept in the museum at the *Maison du Roi* in the Grand' Place.

THE EUROPEAN ECONOMIC COMMUNITY

In contrast to the old buildings of the Grand' Place, the modern headquarters of the European Economic Community proves that Brussels is a contemporary, and important, European capital. The unique, cross-shaped building, located in the neighborhood known as *Berlaymont,* is its administrative headquarters.

The roots of this significant organization date back to 1950, when a French diplomat suggested that some European nations make an agreement to improve international trade in the important steel and coal industries.

As a result of this proposal, the European Coal and Steel Community (ECSC) was established in 1952. The principal agreement reached between the member nations (Belgium, France, Germany, Italy, The Netherlands, and Luxembourg) was to greatly reduce taxes on coal and iron ore trade.

Within a few more years, members of the ECSC were discussing other ways that European nations could help each other develop stronger business ties. In 1957, the EEC was established. The founding nations were identical to those in the ECSC, but the policies of the Common Market were so successful that a number of other countries soon joined the organization. The United Kingdom, Ireland, and Denmark became members in 1972, Greece in 1981, and Spain and Portugal in 1986.

The headquarters of the EEC give Brussels much of its international character. Although more than ten thousand people from various European nations work at the EEC, the organization also has attracted literally hundreds of other international organizations, including the important European Atomic Energy Community (Euratom), a number of chambers of commerce from other nations, and a great many financial institutions. These organizations, like the EEC, bring many people from other nations to the capital of Belgium.

NATO: THE NORTH ATLANTIC TREATY ORGANIZATION

In 1949, when the memories of the devastation of World War II were still fresh, the United States joined eleven other nations in forming the North Atlantic Treaty Organization (NATO). The treaty that was signed by representatives of each member nation declared that an armed attack against any one country would be considered an attack against all. The founding members of NATO were the United States, Canada, Iceland, Belgium, Italy, France, Portugal, Luxembourg, Norway, Great Britain, The Netherlands, and Denmark. Greece and Turkey became members in 1952, West Germany in 1955, and Spain in 1982.

Until 1967, NATO was headquartered in Paris, France. The French government, led by General Charles de Gaulle, announced that NATO headquarters could no longer remain in Paris. NATO was faced with a sudden crisis, but the government of Belgium

NATO headquarters (left) and the Atomium (right), which has an exhibition of peaceful uses of atomic energy and a restaurant

came to the rescue. The other members of NATO accepted the Belgian government's offer to move the organization to Brussels. At the same time, the Supreme Headquarters Allied Powers in Europe (SHAPE), the military command of NATO, also moved to Belgium.

NATO is an enormous organization. Approximately 3.5 million soldiers are stationed under NATO control in various European nations. If any NATO country were attacked, more than twice that many soldiers could be quickly mobilized to defend it. Like the EEC headquarters, the headquarters of NATO brings people from many different lands to Brussels.

A EUROPEAN MASTERPIECE

A map of Brussels looks much like a maze; most of its streets are narrow and crowded, but a few are wide boulevards. Hardly any of them run parallel to one another. A visitor to the city can easily become lost, but nestled along the crooked streets are some

A narrow street that leads into the Grand' Place.

of the most interesting and lovely places to visit in all of Europe.

One of the most unusual buildings is just north of the city. Built for the 1958 Brussels World's Fair, the 335-foot-(102-meter) high Atomium is shaped like a model of a molecule, with spherical atoms surrounding a central atom. Built from small triangles of metal carefully joined to give the illusion of perfect spheres, the oddly shaped building boasts the fastest elevator in Europe in the central column and some of the longest escalators on earth. Inside the Atomium are exhibits depicting scientists who pioneered research on atoms and energy.

From the restaurant at the top of the Atomium, it is possible to see parts of the palace of King Baudouin and Queen Fabiola, Belgium's reigning monarchs. The grounds of the royal palace are beautifully landscaped. On some summer days, the large greenhouses are open to public view.

Considering Belgium's long history as a battleground of kings, it is hardly surprising that there is more than one royal residence in its capital. Toward the center of the city, within walking distance of the Grand' Place, is the *Palais Royal*, the site of the former palace of the dukes of Burgundy and Charles V. The Royal Palace,

*Top: The changing of the guard
in front of the Royal Palace
Above: The Parc de Bruxelles
Right: The twin towers of the
Cathedral of St. Michael*

*Other views of Brussels are a pedestrian mall (left)
and new housing (right) built in the traditional style.*

as the current mansion is called, was built in the eighteenth
century and is at one end of a large and beautiful park, the *Parc de
Bruxelles* (Brussels' Park).

At the other end of the carefully landscaped grounds is
Belgium's Parliament building, called the *Palais de la Nation*,
where the lawmaking assembly meets. A number of rooms in the
Parliament building are open to the public. Other historic
buildings in the area were built during the eighteenth century for
some of the most important noble families in the area. Many now
house government offices.

Brussels is noted for a number of large museums. The Museum
of Ancient Art (*Musée d'Art Ancien*) features paintings by well-
known artists from what is now called the Flemish school,
including Hubert and Jan van Eyck, Hieronymous Bosch, a
number of generations of the Brueghel family, and Peter Paul

Rubens. Brussels' Museum of Modern Art (*Musée d'Art Moderne*), completed in 1986, exhibits works by more contemporary artists.

A third museum in Brussels has displays of artworks from times as ancient as the Biblical era, while a fourth is devoted to exhibits from the military. There is even a museum near the Grand' Place devoted solely to lace cloth. Until the 1600s, Brussels was famed throughout Europe as a center of a huge lacemaking industry, in which as many as fifteen thousand people, mostly women, were employed at one time. At the Lace Museum, visitors can see examples of the finest lace imaginable, as well as old portraits of European monarchs wearing their finest Belgian lace.

Like most other ancient cities in Belgium, Brussels has its share of historic castles and churches. The best known historic churches are the enormous St. Michael's Cathedral and the equally impressive *Notre-Dame du Sablon*. But many of the more than one million people who live in Brussels do not even have to leave their homes or apartments to tour a historic building. Many homes within the city are at least several centuries old. Most of the brick buildings have narrow fronts and are joined at the side to other buildings. Few of the buildings are more than four stories high, since electric elevators did not exist when they were built.

One sight the visitor to Brussels will see little of is the Senne River, which once flowed through the center of the city. For hundreds of years, people erected buildings that partially covered the Senne, and in the 1800s, engineers working for the city decided to cover it completely. Now the river flows underground through a system of tunnels not unlike storm sewers.

The city planners of Brussels, however, have been careful to preserve at least some of the natural beauty of southern Flanders. There are many public parks in Brussels, and the largest is the

The Museum of Modern Art (left) and the Galeries of St. Hubert (right)

12,000-acre (4,857-hectare) Forest of Soignies, which extends from the city all the way to the southern suburb of Waterloo, the famous site of Napoleon's last great battle. Many regard it as the finest and most beautiful city park in the world. The park has something for everyone, including racetracks, boating lakes, trails for cyclists and joggers, fine restaurants, and, most important, miles of unspoiled forests, where deer and other wild animals roam freely, close to the heart of a major city.

So many attractions are packed into Brussels that it is impossible to cover them all. There are a number of large markets, some of them outdoors, where shoppers can buy just about anything. One of them, called the Galeries of St. Hubert, is the oldest covered shopping mall in Europe. More than three dozen theaters present plays in either French or Dutch, and scores of music halls, modern discothèques, and rock music clubs present

Rooftops of Brussels

every kind of music imaginable, from classical symphonies and grand opera to the latest rock hits. Perhaps most important, Brussels is close to everything in Belgium, and not far from other major European capitals as well. Many experienced European travelers use Brussels as a home base for exploring much of Western Europe.

From the charming narrow streets of the central city, to the nearby farmlands and historic cities of Flanders, it is hard to imagine a more fascinating place to visit than Brussels.

Chapter 6

A DIVERSE DEMOCRACY

Belgium is a democracy, even though it has a king who attains his office by succession within the royal family. It is often said that the king reigns but does not rule. Most political leaders are elected by the citizens of Belgium, just as presidents and congressmen are elected in the United States. But there are differences between the elected governments of Belgium and the United States.

On May 29, 1985, the final game of the European Soccer Cup was held in Brussels. The two teams, one from England and the other from Italy, played the game as planned. But as the contest ended, a number of fans, mostly followers of the British team, went on a violent rampage. During the riot, a total of thirty-eight people were killed, the majority of them when a stadium wall collapsed.

The Belgian Parliament, an organization most similar to the United States Congress, immediately began to study the causes of the tragedy. Although the investigation showed that the British team's fans were mostly to blame, Parliament also criticized a member of the Belgian government, the minister of the interior, for not requiring stricter security at the stadium. Many representatives in Parliament called for the resignation of the minister, but he refused. In anger, members of the French-speaking party of Liberty and Progress decided to withdraw their support from Flemish-speaking Prime Minister Wilfried Martens, leader of the Christian Democrat party, and a man with power similar to that of the president of the United States.

On July 16, little more than two weeks after the tragic soccer game, Prime Minister Martens announced to King Baudouin that the government no longer had enough votes in Parliament to govern effectively, and asked for permission to resign. The king, who has little political power except at times of governmental crises, refused to accept the resignation of the government led by Martens. However, he knew that something had to be done quickly. Elections were held for a new government in October 1985.

It is difficult to imagine the government of the United States falling because of the outcome of the Super Bowl, no matter how tragic, but that is just what happened in Belgium. To understand why, it must first be understood how difficult it is to govern the little nation of Belgium.

A GOVERNMENT OF COALITIONS

Between the end of World War II in 1945 and the time when Wilfried Martens became prime minister in 1981, Belgium was led by a total of thirty-one different governments. On the average, the nation had a new government nearly every year during that period. Much of the reason for this is Belgium's voting system, which virtually ensures that most of its major political parties will be represented in Parliament.

From the time all Belgian adult males were given the right to

Wilfried Martens, who became prime minister in 1981, (left) and King Baudouin (right)

vote in 1920, until the 1960s, Belgian voters usually divided themselves between two major political parties, the Social Christian Party (often referred to simply as Catholics, the party was developed to help foster Catholic values) and the Belgian Labor party (known by many as Socialists), as well as the smaller Liberal party, which later changed its name to the party of Liberty and Progress (which has been known as the anti-Catholic party). There was also a small Communist party that got very few votes. In the 1960s, however, under the impact of disputes between Flemings and Walloons, each of these three parties divided itself into separate Dutch- and French-language organizations, and people also began voting for new parties emphasizing the interests of the Flemings, the Walloons, and the French-speaking people of the Brussels area. These developments made the problem of finding a majority that would support a government much more complicated than before.

Because there are so many political parties, no single party controls a majority of representatives in Parliament. It is often necessary, therefore, for parties to join forces to form a government. The result is called a coalition. By working together, two or more political parties can govern the nation effectively, but coalitions are fragile. A number of other European nations are also ruled by coalition governments, but Belgium's different official languages sometimes compound the problem.

In 1972, for example, the local governments of six small towns along the language frontier were switched from Flemish to Walloon administration. A number of politicians were angered over the change, and the national government fell.

Guidelines for the peaceful change of governments are written into the Belgian constitution. When one government falls and a new one comes into power, newspapers and television newscasts cover the stories of the political struggles, but the day-to-day life of average citizens changes little.

In theory, all Belgian citizens over the age of twenty-one are required by law to vote. Anyone who doesn't vote may have to pay a fine, although the fines are not collected often. General elections are scheduled every four years, but special elections are often held when a government falls. A government in power often calls for early elections at a time when it feels it is popular enough to win.

Despite the frequent crises in control of the government, Belgium is a well-run and peaceful nation. The Belgian government is divided into executive, legislative, and judicial branches.

THE EXECUTIVE BRANCH

When Belgians speak of their government, they are usually referring to the executive branch, which is composed of the king and his cabinet ministers. Most cabinet ministers are members of Parliament who have been appointed to the cabinet by the king with the approval of Parliament. Because Parliament must approve the king's appointments, the king must appoint cabinet members who belong to the most powerful political parties in

Parliament. According to a revision in the Belgian constitution made in 1971, the cabinet must have an equal number of French-speaking and Dutch-speaking ministers, with the exception of the prime minister. The prime mininster is the most powerful cabinet member, and usually belongs to the political party with the most members in Parliament.

A government falls when a majority of the members of Parliament no longer support the cabinet. When that happens, politicians often try to develop a new coalition. If that fails, the outgoing prime minister requests that the king dissolve Parliament. If the king follows the suggestion, new elections are held, usually within a few weeks.

The king is commander-in-chief of the armed forces and can declare war and make treaties, but he can only do so with the approval of a cabinet minister. In fact, a cabinet minister must approve virtually all royal acts, including calling and dissolving Parliament, granting pardons to prisoners, and granting titles of nobility. In this way, the power of the king is carefully checked by the nation's system of political parties.

Members of the cabinet sit in Parliament, debate new laws, and cast votes in the name of the king. The principal role of the cabinet is to present a law-making program to Parliament and to advise the king. When a king dies, the cabinet runs the executive branch of government until a new king is crowned.

THE LEGISLATIVE BRANCH

Like the United States Congress, the Belgian Parliament is divided into two houses: the Senate and the Chamber of Representatives. All 212 members of the Chamber of

The Parliament building

Representatives are chosen in elections, but only two-thirds of the 178 members of the Senate are elected. The remaining members are elected by local governments, by the Senate itself, or are members by birthright. The king's sons, as well as princes who could become king, are allowed to be senators. For example, the prince of Liège, the brother of the king, is automatically allowed to sit in the Senate.

The three major responsibilities of Parliament are to make laws, to approve the cabinet, and to help the cabinet formulate policy on major issues. Bills may be introduced by either the executive or the legislative branch of government, but to become a new law, a bill must be approved by both houses of Parliament and signed by the king.

Nearly as important as its lawmaking responsibilities is the right of Parliament to topple a government. Whenever a majority of the members of Parliament no longer feels that the cabinet is operating in the best interests of the nation, it can force the exective branch of government to fall. A vote of "no confidence," as it is often called, usually means that a new government must be created.

For certain cases specified by the constitution, both houses of Parliament are divided into French-language and Dutch-language groups. At all other times, Parliament is a bilingual assembly. Although many members of Parliament speak both Dutch and French, political practice causes almost all representatives to speak in the tongue of their constituency. Headphones are available to hear interpreters translate Dutch to French and vice-versa.

THE JUDICIAL BRANCH

According to the Belgian constitution, the judiciary has equal power with the executive and legislative branches of government. Judges are appointed for life and cannot be removed easily. For this reason, they can perform their duties without worrying about frequent changes in the government caused by party politics.

Members of the judiciary try civil and criminal cases and can rule on whether actions by the executive branch of government are in agreement with Belgian law. Unlike American courts, they cannot rule a law unconstitutional; that responsibility remains with the legislative branch of government. There are a number of different kinds of courts. Three of the courts are established based on the severity of the crime being considered.

Anyone who has to be a defendant in a Belgian court would certainly prefer to appear in police court, sometimes called justice of the peace court, of which there are several hundred in the nation. A justice of the peace acts as judge in these courts, and there are no juries. The maximum penalty that can be given to anyone proved guilty in police court is seven days in jail.

Tribunals are used to try more serious offenses. There are no juries in this court, either. Instead, from one to three judges try

each case. The maximum penalty is five years' imprisonment.

Serious crimes are tried in the nine Superior Courts. The Superior Court is the only court in Belgium that uses the jury system. A Belgian jury can convict a defendant by a simple majority vote. The jury does not have to be unanimous. However, even if a majority of jurors in Superior Court feels that a defendant is guilty, the three judges who sit at each trial may acquit the defendant if they feel the majority voted incorrectly.

The two highest courts in Belgium are the Courts of Appeal and the Court of Cassation. The Courts of Appeal decide whether cases were tried correctly in the lower courts, and try cases involving top government officials. The highest court in the land is the Court of Cassation. At least seven judges sit whenever the Court of Cassation is in session. The primary purposes of the court are to interpret the law and to hear appeals from other courts.

LOCAL GOVERNMENT

There are nine provinces in Belgium. East Flanders, West Flanders, Antwerp, and Limburg are mostly Flemish provinces. Hainaut, Namur, Luxembourg, and Liège are primarily Walloon. The central province of Brabant, home district of Brussels, has territory in both Flanders and Wallonia. A few of the names can be confusing. East Flanders and West Flanders are provinces, but Flanders is also the name of the district that describes all of

Flemish-speaking Belgium north of the language frontier. The province of Luxembourg in Wallonia is not the same as the Grand Duchy of Luxembourg, which is a tiny independent nation that borders the Belgian province of the same name.

Each of the nine Belgian provinces has a provincial council, which deals with interior matters such as road maintenance, some waterway systems, public health matters, and the government of some aspects of local schools. A provincial governor for each province is nominated by the Belgian cabinet ministers and named by the king. Members of provincial councils are not elected officials.

The smallest unit of government in Belgium is the commune. There are nearly seven hundred communes scattered throughout the nation, each administered by a council made up of a mayor as well as a number of councillors and aldermen. Mayors, called *burgomasters*, are officially appointed by the Belgian king, but are always nominated by the local commune council. These councils direct local police offices, control local roads and public utilities, manage fire departments, administer welfare bureaus, and perform other functions directly related to the welfare of the citizens living within the boundaries of the commune.

Because different groups of Belgians have wanted more say in their own affairs, in recent years the constitution has been amended to take away some of the power of the national government and give it to new regional bodies. For dealing with cultural matters, such as education, each of the three language communities acts as a separate body; in addition, Flanders and Wallonia now have regional governments as well. The Brussels region, however, remains under the control of the national government.

A fuel barge passing a steel mill (left) and a chemical plant (right)

THE GOVERNMENT AND EVERYDAY LIFE

The government takes an active role in the daily lives of Belgian citizens. For many years, the wages paid to Belgian workers, as well as the costs of products they buy in stores, have been, at least in part, controlled by the government. Government-operated health insurance is part of the national scene; hospital and doctor bills are paid for nearly everyone. A few of the largest industries in the nation, such as steel and shipbuilding, are owned by the government. The government even requires that persons fired from their jobs be given up to nine months' severance pay.

Of course, all these services have a price. In the early 1980s, when business in Belgium (and much of the rest of the world) was slumping, the government was forced to cut back on some of the benefits Belgians enjoy from their government. Taxes also tend to be high, and many Belgians go to great lengths to avoid paying them. In fact, avoiding taxes is nearly a national pastime. Many Belgians set up tiny companies, with dad as the president, a grandparent as chairman, and children as employees just so that business expenses can be claimed to reduce taxes!

Chapter 7

WALLOONS AND FLEMINGS: SOME FAMOUS BELGIANS

For a country that is smaller than most states in the United States, Belgium has been a fertile ground for famous people, especially in the areas of art and music. Of course, many of the best-known figures lived well before Belgium's independence, at a time when the land that is now Belgium was a battleground for European kings and princes. Nevertheless, modern Belgians regard these historical superstars as part of their national heritage. Especially in the area of art, their effect is still felt over much of the country.

THE FLEMISH MASTERS

Until the development of photography in the nineteenth and twentieth centuries, painting was the most important method of representing people and places. For centuries, many people who could afford an artist's fee had portraits made of themselves and their families. In the fifteenth century, two Flemish painters were instrumental in developing the art of oil painting, and they gave rise to a school of art known as the "Flemish Masters."

From ancient times through the late Middle Ages, most artists used tempera paints. Tempera is made by grinding up solid pigments and dissolving them in water and some other substances, such as egg whites or milk products. Although tempera paints were used for thousands of years, they had many drawbacks. These paints dried very quickly, and tended to change color as they dried. Even skilled artists found it extremely difficult to match old paint with new. For the same reason, it was nearly impossible to produce fine gradations of color, or to smoothly blend tones. Finally, because tempera paints dried quickly, it was nearly impossible to correct errors.

HUBERT AND JAN VAN EYCK

Two brothers born in Flanders in the late 1300s changed the way artists throughout much of the world created their works. The van Eyck brothers dissolved their powdery pigments in oil instead of water. Although this process had been known for many years, few artists had ever tried to work with oil-based paints. The van Eycks discovered that oil paint did not change color as it dried, a process that took many months, even years. It was easy to match old and new colors, to blend colors together, and to fix mistakes by scraping off old paint and painting over the area. As soon as the glorious paintings produced by the van Eycks with their new oil paints were seen by other artists, the technique spread throughout Europe. By the middle of the fifteenth century, almost all artists in Europe were painting with oil-based paint instead of tempera.

The Arnolfini Wedding *(left), painted by Jan van Eyck in 1434, and a statue of the van Eyck brothers (right) in Ghent*

Little is known of the life of Hubert van Eyck, who was born around 1366 and died in 1426. In fact, the only surviving work that he is known to have helped create is the famous *Adoration of the Mystic Lamb,* a work that depicts a number of stories from the Bible. For more than five hundred years, the huge artwork has been on display in the Cathedral of Saint Bavon in the ancient Belgian city of Ghent. Composed of twenty-four separate panels, the masterpiece has left its home only once since its creation in the 1400s. During World War II, Hermann Goering of Hitler's Nazi government stole it and had it shipped to Germany, but it was returned after the war.

Although Hubert van Eyck did some of the early work on the *Adoration of the Mystic Lamb,* he died before it was completed. Jan van Eyck finished the work his brother had begun. Much more is known of Jan's life than that of his brother. Jan van Eyck, who was born around 1370 and died around 1440, spent the last fifteen years or so of his life in the employment of Philip the Good, duke of Burgundy, for whom he created many great paintings. Quite a few of his works still survive. In addition to the "Mystic Lamb" in Ghent, other paintings by Jan van Eyck can be found in the Louvre in Paris, the National Gallery in London, and in the Metropolitan Museum of Art in New York City, among other places.

THE BRUEGHELS

Following the tradition of the Flemish school of oil painting was a family of three famous artists who lived in the sixteenth and seventeenth centuries. The oldest of the three artists was Pieter Brueghel, also known as Pieter the Elder, who was born around 1520 and died in 1569. Although Pieter the Elder was born on land that is now The Netherlands, he studied art in Antwerp and spent the final fifteen years of his life in Antwerp and Brussels. Some of his works, which include scenes from the Bible, portraits, and landscapes of the lovely Flemish countryside, can be seen in major world museums.

Two sons of Pieter the Elder, both born in Brussels, also became famous artists. The eldest son, also named Pieter Brueghel but often called Pieter the Younger, lived from around 1564 to 1638. Some of Pieter Brueghel the Younger's most famous paintings depict frightening visions of the Devil and the fiery regions of hell. The subjects earned him the nickname "Hell Brueghel." He often painted enormous pictures, including Flemish landscapes as well as Biblical subjects.

The younger son of Pieter the Elder was named Jan Brueghel,

The Conversion of St. Paul *by Jan Brueghel*

who lived from 1568 to 1625. Early in his career Jan Brueghel painted still lifes and developed such a smooth technique that he became know as the "Velvet Brueghel." Later, he painted landscapes, portraits, and Biblical scenes, not unlike his father and brother. He also helped his friend Peter Paul Rubens, perhaps the most famous of all the Flemish masters, create some of his paintings.

PETER PAUL RUBENS

The greatest of all the Flemish masters was actually born in Prussia, on land that is now in West Germany, but he was thoroughly Belgian nevertheless. Before his birth, the artist's family had lived in Antwerp, where his father, Johannes Rubens, was a member of the city government. Unfortunately, Johannes also had become a member of the Protestant Calvinist faith at a time when Protestants and Catholics were involved in fierce warfare.

91

A self-portrait (left) and The Miraculous
Draught of Fishes *(right) by Peter Paul Rubens*

To escape the religious battles, the Rubens family moved to land
that is now Germany in 1568. The move may have saved the life
of one of the world's greatest painters. In 1576, the year before
Peter Paul Rubens' birth, thousands of residents of Antwerp were
killed in the religious battle that became known as the "Spanish
Fury." Like thousands of other Flemish people, the family of
Johannes Rubens escaped the slaughter by leaving its homeland.

Peter Paul Rubens was born on June 29, 1577, in a part of
Prussia called Westphalia. When Johannes died ten years later, the
ten-year-old boy and his mother returned to Antwerp, where
Rubens began to study painting with a variety of Flemish artists.
By the end of the century, the twenty-three-year-old artist had
traveled to Italy, where he continued his study with the Italian
masters, including Titian.

Rubens was an extremely well educated man, in addition to
being a masterful artist. He could speak Latin expertly, and had

grown up among the nobility in Prussia and, later, Antwerp and Italy, where he learned to speak like a nobleman. During several periods of his life, he was employed as an ambassador, meeting such people as Philip III and Philip IV, kings of Spain; Archduke Albert and his wife Isabella of Austria; Marie de Médici, queen mother of France; and Charles I, king of England.

But it was for his magnificent paintings that Rubens is best remembered today. Partly because he met so many European kings and queens as an ambassador, he was able to paint portraits of many members of the nobility, including kings of England, France, and Spain. He also painted famous pictures of himself and two wives. His first wife, Isabella, died in 1626. In 1630, at the age of fifty-three, he married his second wife, Helena, who was only sixteen years old at the time. At his enormous studio in Antwerp, Rubens and a small army of assistants and friends, one of whom was Jan Brueghel, created huge artworks that now can be found in major museums throughout much of the world and in priceless private collection in Belgium.

ANDREAS VESALIUS

Little more than a century after the van Eycks revolutionized European art, another Belgian altered forever scientists' understanding of human anatomy. For more than a thousand years, European scholars and doctors had based much of their knowledge of the human body on the work of an ancient Greek physician named Galen, who lived during the second century. Andreas Vesalius, the man who first modernized the centuries-old work of Galen, was born in Brussels in 1514. He was educated at the University of Louvain.

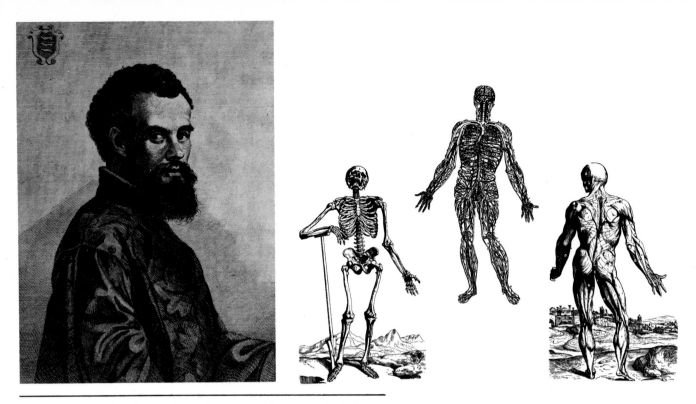

Vesalius (left) and some of his anatomical studies

Like other scholars of his time, Vesalius studied the writings
and illustrations of Galen and compared them to his own studies
of the human body. As important as these studies were, they were
far from pleasant. In order to understand what was inside the
human body, Vesalius knew, he had no choice but to dissect it—
cut it open and examine the organs and tissue under the skin.
Prior to Vesalius's work, many doctors and scientists had
dissected the bodies of animals in order to learn more about
human anatomy.

Vesalius found ways, often around graveyards in the middle of
the night, to get human cadavers that he could dissect and
observe. His studies, and the careful drawings that he and others
made from his notes, showed that the human body was quite
different from the model suggested by Galen. In fact, Vesalius was
able to show that Galen had based his description of the human
body on the dissection of lower animals.

Not surprisingly, Vesalius spent most of his professional life at the center of a storm of controversy. Many people wondered why he wanted so many human bodies. Scientists, who should have understood the importance of his work, were disturbed by his challenges to the work of Galen, who was still regarded as the highest authority on the subject of human anatomy.

The only answer Vesalius had for his critics was to keep moving. He left Belgium for Italy, where he worked at universities in Padua, Pisa, and Bologna. In 1544, he moved to Madrid, Spain, where he became the physician to Emperor Charles V. There he found himself in even greater distress.

In Madrid, Vesalius was accused of dissecting a body before it was completely dead. Because of the accusation, he was directed to make a pilgrimage to Jerusalem, which he began in 1563. He died in Greece on the return trip. The most famous work of the man now called the father of modern anatomy was the seven-volume *De Humani Corporis Fabrica*, Latin for "On the Structure of the Human Body." Many copies of the work, as well as the accurate illustrations it contained, still exist today.

GERARDUS MERCATOR

What Andreas Vesalius did for the science of anatomy, Gerardus Mercator did for the art and science of mapmaking. Like anatomy, mapmaking in Europe was dominated for more than a thousand years by the work of a scientist who lived in the second century. That scientist, Ptolemy, was probably born in Greece but spent much of his life working at the ancient library in Alexandria, Egypt. The maps he made of the earth and the stars were considered the most accurate available until well into the sixteenth century.

The man who finally modernized the maps of Ptolemy was a

Gerardus Mercator

Belgian named Gerardus Mercator, who was born in 1512. Like Vesalius, Mercator studied at the University of Louvain, where he was graduated in August of 1530. Less than ten years later, he completed a large map of Flanders, which still exists at a museum in Antwerp. At about the same time, he completed a map of the world. Unlike the detailed map of Flanders, however, Mercator's map of the world was still much like the one created by Ptolemy nearly fourteen hundred years earlier.

During the religious wars in Flanders, Mercator gradually turned toward Protestantism. Because of his new religion, he was arrested in 1544 along with forty-two other Belgians. Mercator escaped serious harm, but some of the others were not so lucky. Two of the people arrested with him were burned to death, one was beheaded, and two others were buried alive. Not surprisingly, Mercator decided to spend the rest of his life in Germany.

From his new home in Germany, traveling frequently to

Belgium and other European countries, Mercator developed the maps that finally modernized the work of Ptolemy. His enormous map of Europe, published in 1554, showed the size of physical features such as the Mediterranean Sea much more accurately than ever before.

Before he died in 1594, Mercator went on to produce many more maps and globes, depicting both the earth and the stars above more accurately than had ever been done in Europe before. But he is probably best remembered for a style of mapmaking he first produced in a work he completed in 1568. That map used what has come to be known as the "Mercator projection," in which lines of latitude and longitude are shown at right angles.

Since the earth has the shape of a huge ball, on a flat surface it is impossible to accurately depict it. No matter how it is shown, some features will be distorted. Mercator's system expanded the extreme northern and southern portions of the globe so that they could be drawn on a flat surface. The majority of maps of the world today are drawn according to the famous Mercator projection.

THREE FAMOUS BELGIAN MUSICIANS

ADOLPHE SAX

Adolphe Sax was born in 1814 in the city of Dinant, which is in the Meuse River valley deep in Wallonia. Adolphe's father, Charles Joseph Sax, was a well-known maker of musical instruments, and his son more than kept up the tradition. After studying the clarinet and flute at music school in Brussels, Adolphe Sax designed and made the world's first saxophone around 1840.

Like many other Walloons, Sax felt more attached to the French capital of Paris than to the Belgian capital of Brussels. He eventually moved to Paris, where he became an instructor at the Paris Conservatory of Music. During his lifetime, many music critics made fun of the musical instruments he invented. Some of them, such as the saxotromba and the saxhorn, are rarely heard today. But the saxophone, an instrument with a reed mouthpiece and keys like a clarinet but an opening at the end much like a trumpet, became very popular.

At first, the saxophone was used only occasionally in symphony orchestras, primarily by French composers such as Hector Berlioz and George Bizet. But in the twentieth century, American jazz musicians became champions of the new instrument. The saxophone became the most important of all the jazz instruments in dance bands and jazz groups of the middle 1900s. When electric guitars and synthesizers became dominant in rock music, the saxophone declined a bit. But it was given a big boost in the middle 1980s when the rock music superstar Bruce Springsteen featured the lively saxophone solos of Clarence Clemons in a number of hit songs.

CÉSAR FRANCK

Another Walloon musician who chose to live in Paris was the organist and composer César Franck. Born in Liège in 1822, he studied music in his hometown and then at the Paris Conservatory of Music. After spending much of his life in Paris, Franck became a naturalized French citizen at the age of fifty-one.

In Paris, Franck was highly regarded as an expert organist who could make up tunes and variations on the spot. This technique is known as the art of improvisation, which is still frequently used

Left to right: Adolphe Sax, César Franck, Jacques Brel

in all forms of music, especially jazz and rock. He also composed a great deal of music, including operas, chamber and choral music, and a symphony. Most of his music is played only rarely today, but his famous *Symphony in D Minor* is still performed regularly in concert halls throughout the world.

JACQUES BREL

Although he was born in Brussels in 1933 to Flemish parents, Jacques Brel spoke French and seemed to have the soul of a Frenchman. From his earliest years, he began to build a reputation as a singer of French love songs. But by the early 1960s, the character of the songs he composed and sang began to change. Like other folk singers in England and the United States, he became concerned about social injustice and traditional values. Soon, listeners to Belgian radio stations were shocked to hear songs that voiced sometimes unpopular ideas expressed so strongly. In the songs of Jacques Brel, Belgian stations broadcast their first obscenities.

Many listeners were greatly moved by the songs Brel sang. But others were upset by his ideas and sometimes crude language. He soon spent some of his time in Paris, perhaps in part to escape critics who wished to have his works banned. At a performance in Paris, an American musical producer was so moved by his songs that he had them translated into English. He produced the off-Broadway hit musical called "Jacques Brel is Alive and Well and Living in Paris," which is still performed throughout much of the world.

Jacques Brel died in 1979 after a long battle with cancer. But the story of his life, as well as many of the ideals he sang for, are carried on today by his daughter, France Brel. In a suite at a modern shopping center in Brussels, France operates the Jacques Brel Foundation, where visitors can listen to Jacques' music, observe photos and films of him in performance, and hear lectures on topics as diverse as "French Songs of the Twentieth Century," and "The Right to Die in Dignity."

THE MOST FAMOUS WALLOON WHO NEVER LIVED

In the famous detective novels of the English writer Agatha Christie, two characters appear again and again. One is an Englishwoman, Miss Jane Marple. The other is a Belgian policeman, Inspector Hercule Poirot. The fictitious Inspector Poirot was depicted as a heavyset, French-speaking Belgian with a moustache.

In the many books starring the Belgian detective, as well as in dozens of motion pictures and television specials adapted from them, Hercule Poirot interviews many different people as he tries to solve crimes. With wry humor, the author who created Inspector Poirot often gives him a short speech that captures the identity crises faced by so many French-speaking Belgians. "I am Belgian, *monsieur*," the inspector so often says, "not French."

Chapter 8

LIFE AMONG THE
BELGIANS

Since such a long struggle was required for Belgium to become an independent nation, it is perhaps surprising that forces are operating today to split it apart. Years of competition between Wallonia and Flanders have resulted in an increased emphasis on local government. The governments, as well as the day-to-day affairs, of the two regions are becoming increasingly different.

As a result of pressures applied by Flemings and Walloons alike, the Belgian government in 1980 began a process called regionalization. This process has made it increasingly easy for Flanders to be governed primarily by Flemings, and Wallonia by Walloons. Most departments in the cabinet, for example, now have separate offices for Walloon and Fleming affairs. The result is that the two regions are becoming even more separate.

The presence of two such distinct language and cultural groups in one small nation often causes problems for a people with extremely polite public manners. In Brussels, for example, where the two groups often come together, even a casual meeting on a sidewalk or at an outdoor cafe can be difficult. When it is necessary to talk to a stranger, few residents of Brussels feel comfortable. Should a greeting be given in French or in Dutch?

Most experts on manners now suggest that Belgians begin speaking in their native tongue, and hope for the best.

Whether Fleming or Walloon, most Belgians are great handshakers. Among even casual friends and business associates, a long, extended handshake is the rule, both on meeting and parting. Frequently, two or three sets of handshakes are required at the end of a business or social gathering. Historians have suggested that the custom arose years ago, when the land was far less peaceful, so that people could prove they held no weapons in their right hands.

A PROSPEROUS LAND

In Roman times, approximately two thousand years ago, handcrafted products from the Meuse valley were known throughout much of Europe. In more modern times, Belgians have remained world leaders in the field of mechanical engineering. Belgians built the Paris subway system. Belgian machinery and workers have been used to build railways and factories in countries as diverse as Argentina, China, Egypt, Mexico, and Russia. Although it has declined a bit in recent years, as late as 1970 Belgium was rated as the ninth largest industrial power in the world. Today, Belgium still exports more goods per worker than any other nation in the world.

One of the most active exporting industries in the Belgian economy is the chemical industry. Materials such as synthetic fertilizers, petrochemicals, paints and varnishes, soaps and detergents, and rubber and plastic goods are produced in such quantities that approximately 65 percent of the total output of the Belgian chemical industry is exported.

Left: Lace made by machine and by hand   Right: Girls in traditional dress demonstrate the art of lacemaking.

Although not as powerful as it once was, the Belgian textile industry is a significant producer of cotton, wool, and synthetic fibers and cloth. At the beginning of the twentieth century, the textile industry employed one-fourth of the manpower available in Belgium. By the middle of the century, however, the numbers had declined dramatically, principally because many textile operations were moved to countries that paid lower wages than in Belgium. Nevertheless, the Belgian textile industry still exports millions of dollars worth of products each year.

Adding to the wealth of the Belgian economy is its efficient farming system. Although less than 6,000 square miles (15,540 square kilometers) of farmland are available to feed a nation of ten million people, Belgian farmers manage to grow more than 80 percent of the food the nation needs. Prices for farm goods are guaranteed by the Belgian government and the EEC.

The effects of a prosperous economy can be seen almost everywhere. There are few slums in Belgian cities. Belgians are proud of their historic buildings, and preserve many of them with great care. But in the suburbs of large cities, new buildings and homes can be seen almost everywhere.

A byproduct of this wealth is a peculiar custom among Belgian households to stash surprisingly large amounts of cash somewhere in the house. Many foreign visitors are amazed to discover how much money many Belgians can produce almost instantly. Perhaps the custom started from a distrust of banks, or as a way to dodge the tax collector, but it has resulted in an almost comic Belgian practice known as the "guarantee." In many cases when something is rented or borrowed or when, for example, gas or electric utilities are first installed in a household, large cash guarantees are required—and paid without questions.

A LOVE AFFAIR WITH FOOD

Perhaps more than anything else, Belgians are proud of their food. Most are prepared to spend a considerable portion of their income to buy groceries and a large amount of time to prepare their meals. Not surprisingly, they then expect to eat quite leisurely. Until recently in Flanders, it was not unusual for business lunches to last at least two-and-one-half hours. Belgian meals are usually served in many different courses, with plenty of food at each course. The tendency in recent years has been toward somewhat quicker business lunches, but by American standards it is still a very leisurely affair. Belgian schoolchildren often still enjoy lunch breaks lasting between one-and-one-half and two hours. Many Belgians insist that their restaurants offer the finest food

For a meal, a Belgian can shop at a gourmet food store (far left), be entertained while eating at a sidewalk cafe (above), or get something at a fast-food spot (left), such as fries topped with mayonnaise.

in the world, finer even than neighboring France, which also is noted for its cuisine. Foreign visitors often agree, noting that food even in inexpensive restaurants is magnificently prepared.

Some staples of Belgian cooking, however, may require some time for visitors to enjoy. In addition to such familiar dishes as beefsteak, chicken, and fish, Belgian meals often feature eels and mussels. Of the many vegetables served with typical meals, the most famous is certainly the Brussels sprout, a vegetable that looks like a miniature head of cabbage. The hardy Brussels sprout can be grown even during the cold Belgian winters, and has been grown for centuries in small gardens around the capital city.

In their homes, at the finest restaurants, and at little sidewalk cafes, Belgians consume enormous quantities of French fries. *Frites*, as the Belgians call them, are so popular that they are often sold by street-corner vendors, who offer little paper cones filled with fries and topped with mayonnaise.

Two specialties of Belgium are waffles (left) and chocolate (right).

One thing that sets Belgian meals apart from those in
neighboring France is the beer that is often served with them.
While French meals are often accompanied by wine, many
Belgians drink beer with their meals, and at other times as well.
There are more than three hundred varieties of beer in Belgium,
and the Belgians drink more beer than any other national group
except for the Germans. Many outdoor cafes in Belgian cities and
towns serve light meals or snacks with beer, but no other
alcoholic beverages.

Although there is a wide variety of desserts available with
Belgian meals, the best-known sweet in the nation is the superb
Belgian chocolate. At nearly every street corner, vendors sell little
sacks of chocolate that most Belgians insist is superior to any
other in the world.

THE SPORTING LIFE

As for many other European countries, soccer is the most
popular spectator sport in Belgium. It is so popular, in fact, that

Bike racers

sixty-four teams belong to the national soccer league, and even more teams compete on a regional basis. Many Belgian soccer players are not what Americans would call professional athletes. Although they may receive some money for the games they play, many Belgian soccer players, even some of the best known, hold regular jobs in addition to their positions on the teams.

A tourist driving through the Belgian countryside during a warm Sunday afternoon may be surprised to find bicycle races in progress nearly everywhere. Bicycling is the nation's most popular participatory sport, but it is not necessary to race to enjoy outdoor cycling. Many residents ride bicycles to and from work and school, and to explore the cities and countryside. Outdoor maps, especially convenient for cyclists, are posted in numerous spots in many cities and towns, making cycle trips all the easier. Even during the cold Belgian winters, bicycling does not stop. Racers continue their efforts in indoor racetracks, often before sizable crowds. Outdoors, it is not unusual to see Belgian cyclists pedaling right through snowstorms.

On Sunday mornings, a bird market is held in the Grand' Place, Brussels.

Other popular Belgian sports include familiar ones such as tennis, horseback riding, skiing, boating, and hiking. But two other sports may not be so well known to people who do not live in western Europe. One is called sand sailing.

The craft used in sand sailing is called a "sand yacht." The yacht is built with a sail and mast from a sailboat, a body that is little more than a seat, a steering wheel and axles, and wheels like those found on a bicycle. Along the wide beaches of the North Sea, sand yachts can often be spotted speeding along the coast, moved only by the power of the wind.

A second unusual sport, particularly popular in Wallonia, is pigeon racing. Pigeon racing began in Belgium and, particularly on Sunday afternoons, huge races are often held that may cross over three different countries: Spain, France, and Belgium. In some of the most spectacular events, more than 100,000 pigeons may enter a single contest. (Of course, because of their instinct, the pigeons return home.) Birds that have won major races can be worth a small fortune and are sometimes seen for sale on the city streets of Brussels.

THE LAND OF FESTIVALS

No people in the world cherish festivals as much as the Belgians, and there are few places where there are so many. A pamphlet published by a Belgian tourism bureau listed more than seven hundred events, most of them festivals, parades, or fairs of some sort, for the year 1986 alone. It is a rare day when there is not some sort of festival going on somewhere in Belgium.

Some of the nation's most famous festivals have existed for centuries, and many have religious overtones. A number of the best known occur during the Carnival season, the few days leading up to Lent, the period of forty days before Easter when Christians traditionally eat less food and atone for their sins. The most famous of these festivals is the Carnival of Binche, which is held yearly in the little Wallonian city of Binche.

The English word "binge" is thought to come from the name of the town of Binche, and at carnival time it is easy to understand why. Although the entire carnival lasts for three days beginning on a Sunday, the serious festivities start at dawn on Shrove Tuesday (the last day before the beginning of Lent), and continue through the night.

The odd celebration is the one of the strangest sights in Europe. The highlight of the show is the "March of the Gilles." The gilles are men and boys who wear brightly colored padded suits and white hats topped with huge ostrich feathers. The gilles dance down the street, throwing oranges at spectators. Young men who are not in the parade inflate sheep bladders with air and use them to strike anyone unlucky enough not to be wearing a fancy hat.

The carnival probably has its roots in the fifteenth century, when Charles V ruled the land then called the Spanish

Netherlands. During that era, the South American country of Peru was conquered by Spain. Supposedly, the Gilles represent the Inca Indians who were defeated, and the oranges symbolize their gold taken by the Spanish soldiers. During the carnival, the townspeople keep their doors open so that guests can call and have a glass of champagne.

Throughout much of Belgium, the carnival season is a time for merriment. At Blankenberge along the Belgian coast, an elaborate masked ball follows the crowning of a carnival prince at the town hall. A parade of elaborately costumed figures in the town of Aalst in Flanders dates back at least to the year 1435. Dozens of other festivals are held during the carnival season.

Of course, Belgians are far too fond of festivals to restrict them to a single season. Early in July in the magnificent Grand' Place of Brussels, thousands of people dress up in colorful costumes and walk around the square. The festival is called *Ommegang*, which

The Cat Festival in Ypres

literally means "walk around." Although the Ommegang was not celebrated for many centuries, its roots go back at least as far as the middle of the fourteenth century. Today, the festival is enacted according to lengthy notes describing it in the year 1549.

In the Flemish city of Ypres, a Cat Festival is held each May. In the Middle Ages, Ypres was a huge city of perhaps 100,000 inhabitants, larger even than London. According to legend, the city became overrun by rats, and so the townspeople brought in large numbers of cats to control them. Soon the rats were gone but the cats remained, growing even more numerous. Before long, still according to the legend, there were so many cats that the townspeople began throwing them off a tall building called the Cloth Hall. During the modern festival, a parade is held during the afternoon depicting how cats have been worshiped through the ages. In the evening, toy cats are tossed off the ancient building, a mock witch is burned at the stake, and there is a large fireworks show.

A medieval festival in Bruges

Just a few of the other well-known festivals in Belgium are the Parade of Giants in the Wallonian town of Ath, the highly religious Procession of the Holy Blood in Bruges, and the carnival at Nivelles, in which people stage make-believe fights while walking on stilts. These, and dozens of other festivals, have roots that are centuries old.

But there are still other festivals in Belgium, many with more modern origin. Some are devoted to folk, jazz, rock, or classical music, others to art, to nuts, to cheese, and to just about anything else imaginable. In Belgium, a festival can be held for just about any reason—and probably is.

A NATION OF CATHOLICS

When a Belgian refers to the Christian faith, he or she means the Catholic faith. In a nation where at least 90 percent of the population is born Catholic, it is easy to understand why. There are small numbers of Protestants, Jews, and Muslims living in Belgium, and they are allowed to practice their religion openly and without suffering from prejudice. But Belgium remains one of the most strongly Catholic nations in the world. King Baudouin I and Queen Fabiola, Belgium's reigning monarchs, are the heads of the last Catholic royal family in northern Europe.

Not all of the Catholics in Belgium attend mass, especially in Wallonia, but the Catholic church remains an important institution in the nation. A large percentage of Belgian babies are baptized soon after birth. Many marriages take place in the church, although Belgian law requires that a civil ceremony be held as well.

Even during a brief visit to the little European nation, it is impossible to understand it without understanding the Christian faith. Saints and other figures from the Bible and later histories adorn not only the great cathedrals, but also many of the great paintings of the Flemish masters that are scattered throughout more than a dozen important museums and scores of private collections.

THE TINY JEWEL OF EUROPE

For a nation that is only one twenty-fifth the size of Texas, Belgium is astonishingly complex, diversified, and charming. Many European travelers pass through it quickly, on their way to

Faces of Belgium

or from France, West Germany, or The Netherlands. But those who linger inside its modest borders soon learn that all the charms of Europe, including much of its history, are packed into this surprising land.

From the thousand-year-old castles and cathedrals that dot the landscape to the modern skyscrapers of Brussels, there are few places where so much can be seen in such a compact area. Young travelers on a budget can take inexpensive buses and trains everywhere. From Brussels, it is even possible to see much of the countryside on a bicycle. And for the experienced traveler, some of the finest hotels, restaurants, and entertainment spots in the world are also at hand.

The countryside near Ypres

It is also a land that is as difficult to understand as it is easy to enjoy, because Belgium is filled with contradictions. Although it is more like two nations than one, most Belgians, whether Walloon or Fleming, would spare no effort to preserve their country. And while it is true that the French-speaking and Dutch-speaking citizens often bicker, the two cultures also help to enrich the lives of both groups.

In its search for a better and more just society, Belgian leaders and private citizens alike are grappling with one of the world's great problems. How can two groups of people, with often different needs and interests, live together so that each group can flourish? If the Belgians find the answer, they might well find a solution to many of the world's most serious problems.

MAP KEY

Aalst	D4	Hasselt	D5	Oostende (Ostend)	C2
Aarschot	C,D4	Hautes Fagnes (plateau)	D5,6	Ostend (Oostende)	C2
Andenne	D5	Hechtel	C5	Ottignies	D4
Anderlecht	D4	Herentals	C4	Oudenaarde	D3
Antwerp (Antwerpen)	C4	Herstal	D5	Ourthe (river)	D,E5
Antwerp (province)	C4	Hoboken	C4	Overijse	D4
Antwerpen (Antwerp)	C4	Houffalize	D5	Paliseul	E5
Ardennes (mountains)	D,E5	Huy	D5	Peer	C5
Arendonk	C5	Ieper (Ypres)	D2	Péruwelz	D3
Arlon	E5	Izegem	D3	Philippeville	D4
Ath	D3	Jette	D4	Poperinge	D2
Bastogne	D5	Jodoigne	D4	Poppel	C5
Beaumont	D4	Jumet	D4	Puurs	C4
Beauraing	D4	Kinrooi	C5	Recogne	E5
Bertrix	E5	Knokke	C3	Retie	C5
Bilzen	D5	Kontich	C4	Reuland	D6
Blankenberge	C3	Kortrijk (Courtrai)	D3	Rochefort	D5
Bouillon	E5	La Louvière	D4	Roeselare (Roulers)	D3
Brabant (province)	D4	Landen	D5	Ronse	D3
Braine-le-Comte	D4	Lanklaar	C5	Roulers (Roeselare)	D3
Bree	C5	Ledeberg	C3	Saint-Georges	D5
Bruges (Brugge)	C3	Leopoldsburg	C5	Saint-Hubert	D5
Brugge (Bruges)	C3	Lessines	D3	Saint-Vith	D6
Brussels (Bruxelles)	D4	Leuven (Louvain)	D4	Sambre (river)	D4
Bruxelles (Brussels)	D4	Leuze	D3	Schoten	C4
Bullange (Büllingen)	D6	Libramont	E5	Semois (river)	E4,5
Büllingen (Bullange)	D6	Liège	D5	Seraing	D5
Charleroi	D4	Liège (province)	D5	Sint-Amandsberg	C3
Chimay	D4	Lier (Lierre)	C4	Sint-Lenaarts	C4
Comines	D2	Lierneux	D5	Sint-Niklaas	C4
Courtrai (Kortrijk)	D3	Lierre (Lier)	C4	Sint-Truiden	D5
Couvin	D4	Limburg (province)	C,D5	Soignies	D4
De Panne	C2	Lokeren	C3	Spa	D5
Deinze	D3	Lommel	C5	Stavelot	D5
Dendermonde	C4	Lontzen	D5	Terwagne	D5
Deurne	C4	Louvain (Leuven)	D4	Tielt	C3
Diest	D5	Luxembourg (province)	D,E5	Tienen	D4
Diksmuide	C2	Lys (river)	C,D3	Tintigny	E5
Dinant	D4	Maaseik	C5	Tongeren	D5
Dour	D3	Malmédy	D6	Torhout	C3
East Flanders (province)	C,D3,4	Manderfeld	D6	Tournai	D3
Eeklo	C3	Marche-en-Famenne	D5	Turnhout	C4
Ekeren	C4	Mariembourg	D4	Uccle	D4
Emptinne	D5	Martelange	E5	Verviers	D5
Enghien	D4	Mechelen	C4	Veurne	C2
Essen	C4	Meerle	C4	Vielsalm	D5
Eupen	D6	Menen	D3	Vilvoorde	D4
Evergem	C3	Merksem	C4	Virton	E5
Florenville	E5	Merksplas	C4	Visé	D5
Forest	D4	Mettet	D4	Waterloo	D4
Gedinne	E4	Meuse (river)	D4,5	Watervliet	C3
Geel	C4,5	Middelkerke	C2	Watou	D2
Geetbets	D5	Moerbeke	C3	Wavre	D4
Gembloux	D4	Mol	C5	Wellin	D5
Genk	D5	Mons	D3	Werbomont	D5
Gent (Ghent)	C3	Montzen	D5	Wervik	D3
Gentbrugge	C3	Mouscron	D3	West Flanders (province)	C,D2,3
Geraardsbergen	D3	Namur	D4	Westkapelle	C3
Ghent (Gent)	C3	Namur (province)	D4,5	Wevelgem	D3
Gilly	D4	Neerpelt	C5	Ypres (Ieper)	D2
Hainaut (province)	D,E3,4	Neufchateau	E5	Zeebrugge	C3
Halle	D4	Nieuwpoort	C2	Zelzate	C3
Hamme	C4	Ninove	D4	Zomergem	C3
		Nivelles	D4	Zottegem	D3

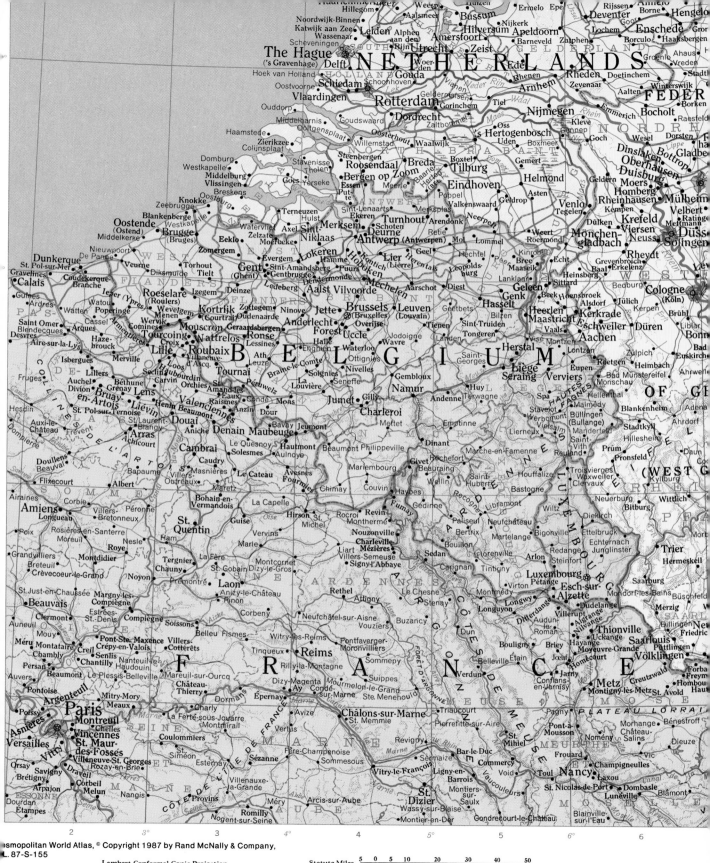

Lambert Conformal Conic Projection
SCALE 1:2,000,000   1 Inch = 32 Statute Miles

Statute Miles
5 0 5 10   20   30   40   50

Kilometers
5 0 5 10   20   30   40   50   60

MINI-FACTS AT A GLANCE

GENERAL INFORMATION

Official Name: Kingdom of Belgium

Capital: Brussels

Official Languages: Dutch and French

Government: Belgium is a constitutional, representative, hereditary monarchy in which the people are sovereign. The monarch, who is head of state, is known as the "king of the Belgians." The king has limited political powers, but plays an important role in choosing a prime minister and serves as an important symbol of national unity.

The cabinet is the executive branch of government; under the revised constitution of 1971, the cabinet must have an equal number of Dutch- and French-speaking ministers.

The Belgian Parliament is composed of two chambers with equal powers. The Senate has 181 members elected by direct vote, by provincial councils, or by the Senate itself. The Chamber of Representatives has 212 members (deputies) directly elected by universal adult suffrage. Both senators and deputies serve four-year terms. Voting is compulsory for citizens twenty-one years old and older.

Provincial councils control interior matters of the provinces. The nine provinces are divided into communes. A communal council is elected and it appoints aldermen to serve with the burgomaster (mayor) in administering the town's affairs.

Religion: Freedom of religion is guaranteed by the constitution. About 98 percent of the Belgian people are Catholics, but few attend church regularly. There are also about 150,000 Protestants and 40,000 Jews. Religion is more important among the Flemish than among the Walloons.

Flag: The national flag was adopted in 1830. It consists of vertical stripes of (from left to right) black, yellow, and red.

Coat of Arms: The Belgian coat of arms is inscribed with the country's motto, *Union Provides Strength,* in both French and Dutch.

National Anthem: "La Brabançonne" ("The Brabant Song")

Money: The basic unit of currency is the Belgian franc. In June, 1989 approximately 42.06 Belgian francs were worth one U.S. dollar.

Weights and Measures: Belgium uses the metric system.

Population: Official estimated 1989 population—9,900,160; 89 percent urban, 11 percent rural. Density, 839 persons per sq. mi. (324 per km²). 1981 census—9,848,647

Major Cities:

Antwerp 483,199
Bruges 117,857
Brussels. 976,536
Charleroi. 210,324
Ghent. 234,251
Liège . . . .'. 201,749
Namur. 103,104

(Population figures based on 1989 official estimates)

GEOGRAPHY

Highest Point: Botrange Mountain 2,275 ft. (693 m)

Lowest Point: Sea level

Rivers: The Schelde, the Sambre, and the Meuse rivers serve as important transportation routes.

Climate: Belgium has a maritime temperate climate. Proximity to the sea brings significant precipitation and moderate temperatures throughout the year. There is an average of 32 to 39 in. (81 to 99 cm) of rain a year. In Brussels the temperature averages 35° F. (1.9° C) in January and 64° F. (17.8° C) in July. Temperatures have a narrower range along the coast and a more extreme range in the Ardennes.

Greatest Distances: East to west—170 mi. (274 km)
North to south—140 mi. (225 km)

Coastline: 39 mi. (63 km)

Area: 11,781 sq. mi. (30,513 km²)

NATURE

Trees: Belgium lies within the area of deciduous forestation. The dominant tree is the oak, and the beech, birch, and elm also are prevalent. The most wooded areas are the Kampenland, where coniferous forests predominate, and the Ardennes, with both deciduous and coniferous trees.

Animals: The animal population is greatly reduced by man's activities. It is Eurasian. Wild boar, wildcats, and deer roam the forests of the Ardennes.

EVERYDAY LIFE

Food: Belgians are big meat eaters; they enjoy beef, chicken, pork, rabbit, and veal. *Carbonades* (beef stewed in beer) and *waterzooi* (a chicken or fish chowder) are two of the most famous dishes. Favorite vegetables include endive, leeks, and white asparagus. Belgians eat many kinds of fish, and eels, cockles, and mussels are considered delicacies. French-fried potatoes are sold at outdoor stands. Cafes are everywhere. The food in Brussels is considered one of the most sophisticated and elegant cuisines in the world. Belgian chocolates and beer are of superb quality.

Housing: There is no housing shortage in Belgium. Most houses are solidly built and have large kitchens that serve as gathering places for closely knit families. Building is encouraged through government loans at low interest rates. Public-housing construction for low-income families is supervised by the National Housing Society. The state is committed to eliminating slum conditions in urban areas.

Holidays:

> New Year's Day, January 1
> Easter Monday
> Labor Day, May 1
> Independence Day, July 21
> All Saints' Day, November 1
> Christmas, December 25

Culture: The Belgian people have a rich cultural history. The most notable heritage can be seen in the painting of Pieter Bruegel the Elder; the music of Orlando di Lasso and César Franck; the plays of Maurice Maeterlinck and Michel de Ghelderode; and in the many palaces, cathedrals, and castles that dot the countryside.

Cultural life in Belgium stagnated during the early years of the nineteenth century, but with the creation of a new artistic and literary review *La Jeune Belgique* in 1882, a vigorous artistic revival began. George Simenon is one of the prolific novelists of the twentieth century and has won world renown. James Ensor, one of the leading Expressionists in Europe, is known throughout the world, also. Frans Maseree and Felicien Rops are among the finest graphic artists in Europe. The surrealist painters Paul Delvaux and René Magritte are outstanding.

Brussels is essentially a Low Country community where the French language became dominant. Its old quarter contains magnificent examples of Gothic and Baroque style. The Theatre de la Monnaie and the Theatre du Parc, the Royal Museum of Fine Arts, the suburban Ixelles Museum of Fine Arts, and the Royal Museum of Art and History with its rich Egyptian collections are among the most important cultural institutions in Europe. The Royal Library and numerous scientific institutions house valuable collections.

A basic cultural diversity exists between the Flemish and the Walloons. In general, the Walloons are attuned to the vibrations of Paris, whereas the Flemings are more concerned with maintaining their own cultural identity without remaining too dependent on the influence of The Netherlands.

Brussels has lost some of its cultural dominance to certain provincial capitals, such as Antwerp, Liège, and Ghent, which have become cradles of contemporary artistic creation, although the National Orchestra in Brussels remains one of the country's most important symphonic ensembles.

Sports and Recreation: Soccer and bicycle racing are the most popular sports in Belgium. Camping in the woods of southeastern Belgium is a popular pastime. North Sea coastal resorts attract many vacationers. In the more rural areas the people enjoy hunting, fishing, and pigeon racing.

Communication: There are over 70 daily newspapers in Belgium, one published in German and the rest in either Dutch or English.

Radio and TV stations are owned and operated by public corporations, which obtain most of their revenues from individual users. One network broadcasts in

French and another in Dutch. Belgians also have access to commercial broadcasting, such as Radio Luxembourg.

Telephone and telegraph lines connect all points.

Transportation: The majority of foreign trade is handled through the port at Antwerp. Brugge-Zeebrugge, Ostend, Ghent, and Brussels are also important ports. Belgian rivers are generally navigable and provide easy access between regions. Many canals connect waterways with each other. In the 1970s Belgium had about 1,000 mi. (1,609 k) of navigable waterways.

In addition to its excellent waterway system, Belgium has well-developed rail and highway networks. Its railway system is one of the densest in Europe. The Société Nationale des Chemins de Fer Belges and the National Interurban Railways are heavily subsidized. Sabena, a government-controlled semiprivate company, has a national monopoly on air travel. Regular helicopter service operates between Brussels and several other continental cities.

Besides automobiles, about 3 million bicycles and a half million motorcycles are in use.

Education: Freedom of education is guaranteed in Belgium, but there have been conflicts between secular and religious schools for centuries. The government provides financial support to both the "official schools," operated by the government, and the "free schools," operated by the church. Education is compulsory for children 6 through 15. Almost all children go to nursery school and kindergarten. Belgium has one of the highest literacy rates in the world. The language of instruction is either French, Dutch or German, depending on the region.

Belgium has several universities: The Catholic University (founded 1425) split into two in the 1960s, with the Dutch-language institution remaining in Louvain and the French-language institution relocated nearby in a new town, Louvain-la-Veuve. It is known throughout the world. The Free Brussels University (1834) is also divided into independent Dutch- and French-speaking universities. The University of Liège (1817) and the State University of Mons (1965) teach in French, while the State University in Ghent (1817) gives instruction in Dutch.

Health: Health insurance, which covers about 95 percent of the population, has had a marked effect on the health of the Belgian people. In addition to the many hospitals, hundreds of centers offer specialized help in medical, geriatric, and psychological areas and in rehabilitation medicine as well.

Principal Products:
Agriculture: barley, cattle, dairy products, flax, hops, oats, potatoes, sugar beets, wheat
Manufacturing: cement, chemicals and chemical products, glass, leather goods, paper, steel, textiles

IMPORTANT DATES

50s B.C.—Caesar leads Roman forces into what is now Belgium and conquers it

A.D. 400s—Clovis, a Frankish nobleman, founds a kingdom that includes Belgium

768-814—Charlemagne rules Belgium. It becomes the center of his empire that covers much of western Europe

900s—The Carolingians lose much of their power; the feudal states develop

1300s and 1400s - The dukes of Burgandy rule the Low Countries

1477—Through marriage the Low Countries come under the rule of the Hapsburgs of Austria

1516—Belgium becomes a possession of Spain

1568-1648—Spanish Netherlands undergoes almost constant warfare

1713—Spain gives Belgium to Austria as part of the settlement of the War of the Spanish Succession

1795—Belgium is annexed by France

1815—Napoleon is defeated at the Battle of Waterloo; Belgium is placed under the rule of The Netherlands

1830—Belgium declares its independence from The Netherlands

1831—Belgium adopts a constitution and chooses as its king Prince Leopold of Saxe-Coburg, uncle of Queen Victoria

1865—King Leopold II succeeds his father

1885—King Leopold II of Belgium establishes the Congo Free State in Africa, later taken over by the Belgian state

1914-18—Belgium fights on the Allied side during World War I and suffers much destruction

1940-45—World War II; fierce fighting takes place in Belgium

1945—Belgium becomes a founding member of the United Nations

1950—Belgium becomes a founding member of the North Atlantic Treaty Organization (NATO)

1957—The European Economic Community is established (EEC)

1960—Belgium grants independence to the Belgian Congo

1962-63—Laws make the language frontier permanent

1967—NATO headquarters are moved to Belgium

1971—The constitution is revised; Belgium is divided into three cultural communities based on language

1980—Flanders and Wallonia are granted partial autonomy by the Belgian Parliament

1989—After years of intense dispute over the national language, the government gives each of the country's three regions power to choose their own language.

IMPORTANT PEOPLE

Albert I (1875-1934), king from 1909 to 1934

Baudouin (1930-   ), king

Hieronymus Bosch, also known as Jerome, (1450-1516), painter of the Flemish school

Jacques Brel (1933-79), folk singer and composer

Adriaen Brouwer (1605-38), Flemish landscape painter

Jan Brueghel (1601-78), Flemish painter

Pieter Brueghel, the Elder (c.1525-69), considered greatest Flemish painter of the sixteenth century

Pieter Brueghel, the Younger (1564-1638), Flemish painter

Cyriel Buysse (1859-1932), playwright and novelist who depicted struggles of peasants against the nobility

Robert Campin (c.1378-1444), Flemish painter

Henri Conscience (1812-83), considered to be creator of the Flemish novel

Charles de Coster (1827-79), author of *Thyl Ulenspiegel*, an account of the Belgian revolt against Spain

Paul Delvaux (1897-   ), modern surrealist painter

François Duquesnoy (1597-1643), Flemish sculptor

Hubert van Eyck (c.1366-1426), painter who worked with his brother Jan

Jan van Eyck (c.1395-1441), painter who with his brother Hubert executed the famous altarpiece, *Adoration of the Mystic Lamb*, now in Ghent

James Ensor (1860-1949), painter and etcher

César Franck (1822-90), Belgian-French organist and composer

Guido Gezelle (1830-99), Flemish poet

Hugo van der Goes (c.1440-1482), Flemish painter

Jacob Jordaens (1593-1678), Flemish painter of scenes of everyday life

Frank Lateur (1871-1969), novelist who depicted primitive passions of the Flemish peasant under the pseudonym of Stijn Streuvels

Camille Lemonnier (1844-1913), novelist

Leopold I (1790-1865), king from 1831 to 1865

Leopold II (1835-1909), king from 1865 to 1909

Leopold III (1901-83), king from 1934 to 1951

Maurice Maeterlinck (1862-1949), essayist, poet, and playwright who combined symbolism and mysticism

Adolphe Martens (1898-1962), playwright who wrote under the pseudonym of Michel de Ghelderode

Hans Memling (c.1430-95), painter of the early Flemish school

Gerardus Mercator (1512-94), Flemish cartographer, known for his Mercator projection

Constant Permeke (1886-1952), sculptor; a leading Flemish expressionist

Dominique Georges Pire (1910-69), winner of the Nobel Peace prize in 1958 for his aid to persons displaced because of World War II

Henri Pirenne (1862-1935), historian

Peter Paul Rubens (1577-1640), Flemish painter of landscapes, portraits, historical, and sacred subjects

Adolph Sax (1814-94), designed the first saxophone

Georges Simenon (1903-   ), prolific writer of detective stories and novels

Paul-Henri Spaak (1899-1972), statesman, head of NATO from 1957-61

Anton Van Dyck (1599-1641), Flemish painter; best known for portraits of the British royal family

Auguste Vermeylen (1872-1945), Flemish critic and author

Andreas Vesalius (1514-64), anatomist; one of the first to dissect the human body, called "father of modern anatomy"

Rogier van der Weyden (1399?-1464), Flemish painter

Karel van de Woestijne (1878-1929), poet

Rik Wouters (1882-1916), sculptor

INDEX

Page numbers that appear in boldface type indicate illustrations

ABOUT THE AUTHOR

Jim Hargrove has worked as a writer and editor for more than 10 years. After serving as an editorial director for three Chicago area publishers, he began a career as an independent writer, preparing a series of books for children. He has contributed to works by nearly 20 different publishers. Some of his Childrens Press titles are *Mark Twain: The Story of Samuel Clemens, Gateway to Freedom: The Story of the Statue of Liberty and Ellis Island, The Story of the Black Hawk War,* and *Microcomputers at Work.* With his wife and teenage daughter, he lives in a small Illinois town near the Wisconsin border.